*Politics and the Regulatory Agencies*

# Politics and the Regulatory Agencies

## WILLIAM Lucius CARY

Dwight Professor of Law, Columbia University

Former Chairman, Securities and Exchange

Commission, Washington, D.C.

McGRAW-HILL BOOK COMPANY

New York          St. Louis          San Francisco
London            Toronto            Sydney

*To*
Katherine, Linn, and Katrina

# The Thomas M. Cooley Lectures
## Sixteenth Series

DELIVERED AT THE UNIVERSITY OF MICHIGAN
FEBRUARY 22, 23, 24 AND MARCH 2, 1966

THE Thomas M. Cooley Lectureship was established for the purpose of stimulating legal research and presenting its results in the form of public lectures. Thomas M. Cooley, for whom the lectureship was named, was a member of the first faculty of the University of Michigan Law School, when it was organized in 1859, and subsequently became its Dean. At the time of his death in 1898 he was one of the most distinguished legal scholars of this country. These lectures are made possible through the endowment for legal research at the University of Michigan, established by the will of the late William W. Cook, a member of the New York bar and an alumnus of the University of Michigan.

# *Preface*

THIS book was stimulated by an invitation to give the Cooley Lectures at the University of Michigan in February of 1966. It is an attempt to present the Federal regulatory commissions in their political context—through my own personal impressions and experiences (as Chairman of the SEC from March 1961 to August 1964) and the observations of my colleagues (commissioners of other agencies). A teacher of corporation law and taxation, I cannot claim expertise either as a political scientist or as a student of administrative law. Rather I am writing as a "bureaucrat" during the brief years of President Kennedy's and the first phase of President Johnson's administration.

❊  ❊  ❊

To the law students I have a special message. My conclusions here are orthodox, offering no formula on which Federal regulatory agencies may be revolutionized. When I was your age, I confess that I was not only a reformer, but an evangelist. My ardor has been tempered, but I trust not arrested, by political realities. Wall Street is not one hundred percent dragon, and—unhappily—a St. George in Washington might perhaps resemble Don Quixote. Let us bear in mind a quotation from Karl Llewellyn:

Technique without ideals is a menace, ideals without technique are a mess.

❊  ❊  ❊

I am grateful for the criticism of this manuscript by students in the field of administrative law, particularly Carl A. Auerbach, Milton H. Cohen, Roger Cramton, Kenneth C. Davis, Arthur Fleischer, Jr., Hon. Henry J. Friendly, Walter Gellhorn, William K. Jones, Philip A. Loomis, Jr., Nathaniel L. Nathanson, Frank C. Newman, Morgan Shipman, Telford Taylor, and Joseph L. Weiner.

*William L. Cary*

# Contents

# Introduction

TWO WEEKS before I resigned from the Securities and Exchange Commission, when our bill was being voted upon in the House, a friendly Congressman speaking on its behalf paid us one of the highest accolades an agency can expect: [1] "There has never been the least scandal attached to the . . . Commission." Undoubtedly, in his mind this was a compliment. Should we have been pleased with it, or embarrassed? The standard might be higher—whether we have done anything constructive. Ideally, an honest though pedestrian administration scarcely seems enough.

But perhaps this is too much to ask of a regulatory agency and of government generally. Do we expect a commission always to retain its vitality and momentum? I am pessimistic. I do not entertain the illusion that it can. From the very moment I became involved with the SEC I was haunted by two remarks that had been made half seriously. One was by Justice Douglas, that every administrative agency should be dissolved at the end of ten years. The other, even more an exaggeration, has been made by several experts, including Professors Marver Bernstein [2] and Louis L.

---

[1] 110 CONG. REC. 17922 (1964).
[2] BERNSTEIN, REGULATING BUSINESS BY INDEPENDENT COMMISSIONS, 74–95 (Princeton University Press, 1955), [hereafter referred to as Bernstein].

1

Jaffe [3] and Judge Henry J. Friendly.[4] It can be condensed in the salty phrases of Professor John K. Galbraith: [5] "Regulatory bodies, like the people who comprise them, have a marked life cycle. In youth they are vigorous, aggressive, evangelistic, and even intolerant. Later they mellow, and in old age—after a matter of ten or fifteen years—they become, with some exceptions, either an arm of the industry they are regulating or senile."

Of course, I do not accept these comments at face value. Following the ebb there may again be a flow. Regulatory agencies are no different from the Federal departments, of State, Treasury, Defense, or Justice. Secretary McNamara's imaginative reshaping of the Defense Department is an example on a broad scale. Yet the grain of plausibility in these two remarks is that revitalization in every government agency is needed. Continuous administration of acts involving any industry can lead to channelized thinking, loss of excitement, and with it loss of intellectually excited personnel.

Let us then turn to analyze the forces at work upon a commission. How can one keep away from a run-of-mine administration of a regulatory agency? I fear that in some eras that is about all we can anticipate. At times in the course of administrations, whether Democratic or Republican, the only—indeed the highest—goal expected of any agency seems to be that it conduct its day-to-day work honestly without "getting into any trouble." In a political world even that may be high praise, but it offers to the agency only a dusty road for its horizon. The narrower question then, is whether or not more is possible, or more specifically, was possible in the year 1961 when John F. Kennedy became President. For this question to be answered affirmatively, the time must be ripe for new ideas, for obtaining an adequate budget, for generating enthusiasm among the staff and prospective recruits, and for some reasonable acceptance by the industry.

[3] Jaffe, The Effective Limits of the Administrative Process: A Reevaluation, 67 HARV. L. REV. 1105, 1109 (1954).
[4] H. J. Friendly, A Look at the Federal Administrative Agencies, 60 COLUM. L. REV. 429, at 440 (1960); see generally FRIENDLY, THE FEDERAL ADMINISTRATIVE AGENCIES (Harvard University Press, 1962), [hereafter referred to as FRIENDLY.]
[5] GALBRAITH, THE GREAT CRASH, 171 (Houghton Mifflin, 1955).

In attempting to deal with these problems I shall perforce focus primarily upon the Securities and Exchange Commission during 1961 to 1964. At the same time, however, I shall make reference to other agencies, namely, the Civil Aeronautics Board (CAB), the Federal Communications Commission (FCC), the Federal Power Commission (FPC), the Federal Trade Commission (FTC), and the Interstate Commerce Commission (ICC), and occasionally others which may not be "independent" agencies at all. From the so-called "Big Seven" I exclude only the National Labor Relations Board, which has a different—cross-industry— function and a divided administration (i.e., between the general counsel and the Board). The regulatory commissions have such a broad impact upon business that they have sometimes been attacked as the headless fourth branch of the government.[6] To some extent these six (including the Securities and Exchange Commission) have a common role: they are nominally "independent"—a subject for further discussion below—and were created to regulate either one industry or phases of several industries. There was a time when the independent regulatory agencies were being hailed as the saviors of our economic liberties.[7] Now we recognize that they have their own special problems in performing their role. Most of them do their job through several different channels; namely, adjudication of cases, enforcement proceedings in the courts, and rule making—in effect, legislating—under authority of special statutes. Yet they are by no means fungible, a dangerous oversimplification on the part of anyone attempting to lump them together. By way of illustration, some of these agencies are engaged in promoting the industry they regulate: for example, the CAB. Some donate great property rights through licensing: certificates of convenience and necessity, by the FPC; television franchises, by the FCC; and air routes, by the CAB. In political terms these three agencies may be subject to greater stress because they have so much to give away. Their mandate is to protect the public, often against enormous political

[6] See President's Commission on Administrative Management-Report (1937).
[7] See address by James M. Landis quoted in GELLHORN, INDIVIDUAL FREEDOM AND GOVERNMENTAL RESTRAINTS, 5–6 (Louisiana State University Press, 1956).

3

pressure from business and without any countervailing pressures. Occasionally an agency such as the Federal Power Commission in a proceeding involving gas rates has the views of a consumer lobby, such as the state or city government of the area where the gas will be sold. But in other instances, such as the grant of television licenses, there is really no well-defined spokesman for the public except the agency itself. I recognize that the SEC is unique in several respects: it does not give away property rights, and has not actually engaged in the fixing of rates (though the power may exist). Nor is it an arbiter between competitors, as is the ICC.

Before reaching the theme of this book—specifically, the viability of an agency in its political context—we might inquire generally what are the obstacles and forces that affect a commission. Most important of the influences at work upon a regulatory agency are the White House, on one hand, and Congress, on the other. Government regulatory commissions are often referred to as "independent" agencies, but this cannot be taken at face value by anyone who has ever had any experience in Washington. In fact, government regulatory agencies are stepchildren whose custody is contested by both Congress and the Executive, but without very much affection from either one. Furthermore, as stepchildren they are often starvelings, receiving only the crumbs in the Federal budget. Even in 1965, the budget of the six totaled only 96 million dollars in a national budget of 96 billion—0.1 percent.[8] Without the cooperation of both Congress and the Executive, little constructive can be achieved. To reemphasize the point, an agency is literally helpless if either branch is uninterested or unwilling to lend support.

This brings us, first, to an intensive analysis of the relations between the "independent" agency and the White House.

---

[8] Budget of the U.S. Government for Fiscal Year Ending June 30, 1967, pp. 327–343. The amount for each agency under consideration for 1965 was:      (000 omitted)

| | | | |
|---|---|---|---|
| CAB | $11,205 | FTC | $13,662 |
| FCC | $16,747 | ICC | $26,491 |
| FPC | $12,992 | SEC | $15,276 |

The NLRB figure was $25,221,000.

 *The White House*

## What Is the "White House" and Its Attitude?

What is the "White House," as the country becomes more complex and the problems before the President are multiplied? To the agencies it is a different institution in different eras. Today it is a collection of persons, some excellent and some marginal.

In the 1930s many of the regulatory agencies, with the exception of the Interstate Commerce Commission and the Federal Trade Commission, were either born or given new life, during the administration of President Franklin D. Roosevelt. Indeed, the SEC received its charter in 1934, its work having been administered for a year by the Federal Trade Commission. One of the principal interests of President Roosevelt was, in fact, the need for financial reform even while he was Governor of New York. After his inauguration he recommended legislation for "federal supervision of traffic in investment securities" in his address to the Seventy-third Congress on March 29, 1933,[1] and worked directly with the first three chairmen of the SEC (Joseph P. Kennedy, James M. Landis, and William O. Douglas) in carrying forward its policies.[2] As Mr. Landis said in his letter of resignation, "Our

---

[1] The Public Papers and Addresses of Franklin D. Roosevelt, vol. II (1938), (The Year of Crisis, 1933), pp. 93–94.
[2] See generally R. F DE BEDTS, THE NEW DEAL'S SEC: The Formative Years (Columbia University Press, 1964).

commission and our work sprang from your mind, your utterances, your ideals."[3] Federal securities legislation was first enacted as a result of the public sentiment aroused by practices under which securities had been distributed in the 1920s. In the words of Congress:[4] "Fully half or twenty-five billion dollars' worth of securities floated during this period have been proved to be worthless. . . . The flotation of such a mass of essentially fraudulent securities was made possible because of the complete abandonment by many underwriters and dealers in securities of those standards of fair, honest and prudent dealing that should be basic to the encouragement of investment in any enterprise."

At almost the same time, additional impetus was given to other regulatory agencies. The FCC was organized under the Communications Act of 1934. The Natural Gas Act, administered by the FPC, was enacted in 1938. The CAB (then the Civil Aeronautics Authority) was established in the same year. In dealing with the regulatory agencies, therefore, the "White House" at that time was frequently President Roosevelt himself. In attempting to resolve the plight of the railroads he worked closely with Commissioner Joseph B. Eastman, who became the Federal Coordinator of Transportation, rather than with the ICC.[5]

By the time of the war, however, the close ties of the early thirties had loosened and the President was no longer directly involved with the commissions. It is true that in the Truman period the President occasionally saw the Chairman of the SEC but on the basis of personal friendship more than a direct interest in the agency. In general, this attitude carried over through the period of President Eisenhower, whose lack of interest in the regulatory agencies was equaled only by that of his predecessor. This was particularly true after the Democrats won control of Congress. Probably the most influential voice in this field was George M. Humphrey, then Secretary of the Treasury. There was a clearly understood philosophy against further and deeper gov-

---

[3] Commercial and Financial Chronicle, Sept. 18, 1937, p. 1830; quoted in DE BEDTS, op. cit., p. 205.

[4] H.R. 85, 73d Cong., 1st Sess. (1933), p. 2.

[5] See LATHAM, THE POLITICS OF RAILROAD COORDINATION 1933–1936, p. 151 (Harvard University Press, 1959); BERNSTEIN, p. 60.

ernment involvement in business, which reflected itself in continuing thin budgets.

This brings us to the question of what the White House was in the administration of President Kennedy, and of President Johnson in 1964. During the years 1961 to 1963 I never saw the President officially—which surprised many journalists. Actually, at the time of the severe market break in early 1962, I was invited to a conference in the White House with the Secretary of the Treasury, the Chairman of the Council of Economic Advisers, and the Chairman of the Federal Reserve Board, but it was agreed that we should send an alternate since I was scheduled to appear before the House Interstate and Foreign Commerce Committee at the same time: Congress always received precedence despite the importance of the occasion. Perhaps by way of rationalization on my part, the failure to see the President can be treated not as criticism but almost as a compliment. As one of the assistants said: "You would have heard from us if there was anything wrong." The President had no time for, and indeed in the normal course should devote no time to, our problems unless there was "trouble." President Johnson demonstrated more personal sensitivity to the work of the agency, but in both cases it can be said that their focus was, and should have been, on foreign affairs, defense, and getting major bills through Congress.

To a regulatory agency, therefore, the White House was a collection of people, and to most of us it was primarily Ralph A. Dungan, an able assistant who participated in choosing us. Even Mr. Dungan was so heavily involved in matters of greater national and political importance (such as the Foreign Aid program) that he literally had no free time to talk with us. There were, in addition, the equally brilliant but equally busy assistant counsel in the White House, and the Bureau of the Budget, an arm of the Executive. There were also a number of second-echelon political assistants who telephoned, but the brief conversations with them quickly warned one of the danger of becoming too intimate. Every institution, including the office of the President, has its satellites who would like to use their base for the extension of personal power, and their influence is something to be carefully avoided.

7

In view of the fact that most of us rarely saw President Kennedy, why did we chairmen of regulatory agencies feel that there was any encouragement from the White House? Perhaps one of the major reasons was that some of us were appointed without any political ties or commitments—some from universities. Furthermore, the person charged with appointments in the White House gave us encouragement to believe we were there to make things better. During the Kennedy era particularly there was a spirit of reform in the air, not entirely for idealistic reasons. The regulatory agencies had been subject to so much criticism and the ethics of commissioners had been so widely questioned that there was no alternative for any responsible President except to improve their standing.[6] Finally, the encouragement came to us in an oblique but nevertheless concrete form: the Bureau of the Budget took our requests for funds seriously and was willing to approve substantial increases in our budget.

A question arises as to what extent the White House can and should be interested in the regulatory agencies. As a practical matter, even excellent administration of the commissions will probably not help the President much politically. Renovation might yield political capital if the recent history of the agency had been unsavory. In other words, if a commissioner of the Federal Communications Commission had been accused of receiving payments for attempting to influence an award of a TV channel, as occurred in March of 1958,[7] and if criticism were being leveled at other commissions and commissioners, a new policy of quality appointments would be a wise step politically as well as ethically. In general, however, it can be said that the White House is interested and involved in a regulatory agency only if there has been a scandal or wide newspaper publicity about the industry it regulates. On the other hand, one thing is certain: that although the operation of a regulatory agency above pedestrian standards has

[6] The investigation which attracted the most attention in recent years was undertaken by the Special Committee on Legislative Oversight of the House Committee on Interstate and Foreign Commerce. It was established in early 1957 with the sponsorship of Speaker Sam Rayburn. See 103 CONG. REC. 5503 (1957); GELLHORN & BYSE, ADMINISTRATIVE LAW: CASES AND COMMENTS, p. 179 (4th ed. 1960).
[7] This involved FCC Commissioner Richard A. Mack. See N.Y. Times, March 4, 1958, p. 1, col. 1.

very little political appeal, the White House can be very seriously hurt if there is any trouble. It is at that point that the assistants in the White House or even the President himself would become directly interested.

The foregoing generalizations concerning the participation of the White House in the activities of regulatory agencies are by no means novel. After all, in a government of such multifold activities as our own today, the White House can only be interested in a given number of problems. The Executive Office is human, despite the tireless involvement of President Johnson in the myriad details of domestic as well as foreign affairs.

### Formal Controls by the White House

As will appear in Chapter 2, there is a sensitivity on the part of Congress to the powers that the White House may exercise in relation to regulatory agencies. First among them is the power to appoint a chairman from the commissioners and to choose commissioners as their terms expire. As a general rule, appointments are more important in the beginning of an administration because they set the tone. In all probability a chairman may be demoted to commissioner without cause, though the practice is infrequent. During my three and a half years, the ousting of one chairman (of the Federal Maritime Commission) took place in August of 1963 [8] allegedly because he would not take strong action on ocean freight rates said to be detrimental to the export trade. In 1962 doubts were being raised as to whether the able Chairman of the CAB, Alan Boyd, would be reappointed because of opposition from political leaders of the Northeastern region (including Speaker McCormack and Senator Edward Kennedy).[9] Mr. Boyd had taken a stand against permitting Northeast Airlines to retain its route. However, at a meeting attended by all the regulatory heads in the White House President Johnson relieved the tension by announcing that he had decided to reappoint Mr. Boyd. The President's failure to reappoint Joseph C. Swidler as Chairman of the FPC will be discussed later (Chapter 3; Obstacles to Vitality, page 62).

On the appointment of commissioners the President's authority

---

[8] See N.Y. Times, Aug. 25, 1963, p. 84, col. 3; Aug. 27, 1963, p. 62, col. 6.
[9] See *Reform for Regulatory Agencies*, Washington Star, Oct. 15, 1963.

is almost total. In only a very few cases has confirmation been withheld by the Senate. The President is strongly influenced by pressure from Congress and sometimes by his sensitivity to the press. The latter is not always permitted to prevail, however, as demonstrated by newspaper criticism in connection with the 1964 appointment of one of my colleagues.[10] Though he would be the first to acknowledge conservative Republican leanings, his selection was characterized, erroneously as it proved, as a calculated step toward devitalizing the Commission. It is an asset to have another colleague of high integrity.

Appointments are not a matter in which the chairman of a commission has any right to be consulted, but I took the position that the selection of my colleagues was something in which I would like to exert as much influence as possible. One of my fellow chairmen, of far greater political sophistication, said this was a White House prerogative and he would not volunteer his views, but it seemed to me that if we had a program and could obtain support through the selection of a high-grade commissioner, it was my duty to try to bring it about. I did contribute to the appointment of a superior lawyer and former student as a Republican member of the SEC, and strongly urged the reappointment of two outstanding career civil servants (one of them my successor as chairman).

As to removal of commissioners (as distinguished from demoting the chairman), there is no express limitation on the power of the President in connection with the FCC, FPC, and SEC as well as other agencies. However, doubts as to legal power, coupled with the political inadvisability of such a traumatic step, reduce the efficacy of this form of Presidential control.

The authority that the White House may exercise through the appointment of the chairmen and the commissioners, and perhaps over major personnel selections, directly raises the question of personal independence (as distinguished from the independence of the agency itself). Much has been made of the danger of entertainment by the industry regulated, but the problem is deeper. It rests basically on the question of personal security. Do

---

[10] Editorial, *An Unprofessional Appointment*, N.Y. Times, June 9, 1964; Editorial, Washington Post, June 25, 1964; Childs, Washington Post, June 15, 1965.

they want to be liked? Or do they seek power? Do they look for a further career in the administration? And what are they going to do when they leave? Do they plan to work for the industry? If so, some commissioners may feel that they probably should not be too severe in their views, although I found that a company with which I was very strict, though I trust fair, wanted me as its chief executive officer when I left. Another intangible element of personal security is whether a particular commissioner wants to be a judge and therefore may not feel free with counsel who are powerful lobbyists or with their clients who exert a wide influence. Some of the Washington lawyers have developed a remarkably subtle method of exposing the source of their power without threatening to exercise it. Perhaps this problem of personal independence can best be summarized in the response to a question addressed to Newton Minow in 1961: "Just what makes you think you are qualified to be Chairman of the FCC?" "Two things, first, I'm not looking for a job in the communications business, and second, I don't want to be reappointed." [11]

A second form of control by the White House over the regulatory agencies is through the budget. As indicated earlier, the regulatory agencies have been traditionally starved for funds. As Commissioner Rossbach said in a letter to the *New York Times* (April 22, 1954): [12] "In the last seven years the Commission has been undergoing a budgetary squeeze that has drained most of its vitality." Congress was certainly not the only institution responsible for the decline. The White House itself demonstrated indifference or a well-defined policy of cutting back. For the fiscal year ending June 1960, five of the six major commissions received appropriations ranging from roughly seven to eleven million dollars; only the ICC approached twenty million dollars. James M. Landis had pointed out in his 1960 report [13] that

A period of economic rigor, if not parsimony, seems to have characterized the Bureau of the Budget's attitude toward the various

[11] MINOW, EQUAL TIME: THE PRIVATE BROADCASTER AND THE PUBLIC MARKET, p. 45 (Atheneum 1964).

[12] N.Y. Times, April 22, 1954, p. 28, col. 6.

[13] *Report on Regulatory Agencies to the President Elect*, submitted to the Senate Committee on the Judiciary, 86th Cong., 2nd Sess. (Dec. 1960), p. 6, [hereafter referred to as the *Landis Report*].

agencies beginning in 1952, an attitude that was slowly being relaxed in 1960. . . . Obviously, either extravagance characterized the situation in 1950 or parsimony in 1960.

In the budget more than in any other place the attitude of the White House can be reflected, through the approach taken by the Bureau of the Budget. On a day-to-day basis, it is the Cerberus at the gate of any program. Every item has to pass through it, and no request for funds can be made without its blessing. Thus this agency is one of the most pivotal institutions in the government.

Coupled with the budget is the power to allocate supergrades vested in the Civil Service Commission. Any agency that is moving ahead needs able recruits and more places which they can fill at the top. Without them, it is paralyzed.

The final major control that can be exercised by the White House over an independent regulatory agency is with respect to substantive legislation. The control is strict over both detail and policy. Again all proposals must be sifted through the Bureau of the Budget for ultimate approval by the White House, and despite the jealousy that Congress may exhibit over White House participation in an agency's functioning, it is unlikely to enact constructive legislation on behalf of a regulatory agency unless it has some backing from the President. There are several classes of priority employed by the Bureau of the Budget, but one Senate aide has said they make little difference, unless of course the President endorses a bill in his message or otherwise singles it out. This subject will be developed in Chapter 4.

One of the functions which the Bureau of the Budget might be expected to fulfill is to reconcile the differences between agencies on legislation. The clearing-house role of the Budget Bureau was most helpful in one phase of the Securities Act Amendments of 1964.[14] The Department of Justice expressed concern over certain constitutional (delegation) and antitrust difficulties which we successfully overcame after extended discussion. On the other hand, the absence of White House control where even Congress might have anticipated it is demonstrated by the problems which the Securities and Exchange Commission had with the Comptrol-

---

[14] Pub. L. No. 467, 88th Cong., 2d Sess. (Aug. 20, 1964).

ler of the Currency during the years 1963 and 1964 (see Chapter 4; Obstacles in the House, pages 99 to 103).

There are other forms of influence which the White House may exercise. One is over appointments to high positions in the agency. There is an informal understanding as to clearance which some of us felt we could not ignore in more than one or two instances. Policies of selection vary widely in different administrations. I can say that during the Kennedy era most of my chairman colleagues and I had relatively little interference from the White House in this regard, although we were not unaware of the influence which persons on Capitol Hill would have liked to bring to bear. I cannot affirm that this would have lasted as reelection became an imminent issue. Suffice it to say, a great deal of pressure in this area comes from congressmen, either directly or obliquely through assistants in the White House with whom they deal regularly. In my own case, clearance of one appointment was denied just before my departure, but it came so close to the installation of my successor that I could not in good conscience raise objection.

### Degrees of Dependence on, and Independence from, the White House: Where Should the Line be Drawn?

As already indicated, the truly independent regulatory agency often seems but an illusion in the light of experience in Washington. On the other hand, it is not without substance, thanks in part to the attitude of Congress and of appointed commissioners themselves.

(1) An excellent demonstration of the dangers to a chairman or commissioner in responding to pressure from the White House occurred during the Eisenhower administration. One of the major political controversies of that era involved the so-called Dixon-Yates contract for the joint construction and operation by two large private utility companies of a power facility in the Tennessee valley, in lieu of further expansion by the TVA. The press carried it as an issue of public versus private ownership. The contract was subsequently abrogated by the government, and the claim for damages was defended on the ground of conflict of interest, because Mr. Adolphe Wenzell, an officer of the First Bos-

13

ton Corporation, served both as financial agent for the Dixon-Yates combine and as (an unpaid) consultant for the Bureau of the Budget.[15] One of the numerous conditions to carrying out the Dixon-Yates proposal was SEC approval of the financing plan of the two utilities, which were subject to its jurisdiction under the Public Utility Holding Company Act. In June of 1955 a hearing on this subject was in progress before a trial examiner of the SEC when the Chairman of the Commission received a telephone call from Governor Sherman Adams, then presidential assistant to President Eisenhower, on a Saturday afternoon.[16] Governor Adams' special concern at the time was that Mr. Wenzell was expected to testify on the following Monday and to be cross-examined on the subject of the conflict of interest. It was the wrong time from a political standpoint. Debate had already been scheduled in Congress. He said that certain government attorneys interested in the proceeding (actually the Attorney General and the President's counsel) were away from the city, and they wanted an opportunity to determine whether the United States government might wish to intervene. He also said, "I have another problem to worry about this week, namely the TVA appropriation coming up in the House of Representatives," to which the Chairman replied, "That doesn't concern me."

On Monday morning the Chairman conveyed to the full Commission Governor Adams' request that the SEC hearing on Monday be postponed, on the specific ground that the government attorneys were away from the city, and the request was granted. This was brought out in an extensive investigation by a subcommittee of the Committee on the Judiciary of the Senate, and in extended colloquies on the Senate floor (in May of 1957) which can be condensed in the following excerpt: [17]

MR. CARROLL. Is the Securities and Exchange Commission an arm of Congress?

[15] See *United States v. Mississippi Valley Generating Co.*, 364 U.S. 520 (1961).
[16] See *Hearings Before the Subcommittee on Anti-trust and Monopoly of the Senate Committee on the Judiciary*, 84th Cong., 1st Sess., pursuant to S. Res. 61 [Power Policy—Dixon-Yates Contract, pt. I], pp. 415–431 (June–July, 1955).
[17] 103 Cong. Rec. 7512 (1957).

14

MR. KEFAUVER. The Securities and Exchange Commission is an arm of Congress, charged with the duty of enforcing and carrying out in a judicial manner the . . . act.

MR. CARROLL. So actually, if I interpret correctly the statement of the Senator from Tennessee, if the Sherman Adams was the Sherman Adams I have in mind, the Presidential assistant at the White House, he belongs to the executive branch of the Government. Here was a case of the executive branch of the Government interfering with a quasi-judicial function of the Securities and Exchange Commission, which is an arm of Congress, to get a continuance, not from the trial examiner, but from the Chairman of the Commission himself, who would ultimately have to pass upon the decision of the trial examiner.

This colloquy took place more than a year before Governor Adams was forced to resign (in September of 1958).

The question might well be asked of any commissioner what he would do if the spokesman for the President in domestic affairs (in effect, the deputy President) asked him merely to postpone a hearing. I was happy to have this precedent before me when I once received a call from a middle-echelon White House assistant asking me to consider the implications of taking action against a particular well-known promoter. I was able to ask him whether he had ever heard of Sherman Adams, and outlined this event, which immediately terminated the discussion.

As a conceptual matter the Sherman Adams incident raises a borderline question involving independence. There was no suggestion that the Commission or any of its members should take a particular position. The request was only for an adjournment. The Commission Chairman was criticized on other grounds by a Senate committee. But the basic point of attack was that requests for postponement are traditionally made to the trial examiner in the hearing itself, while this request came from outside, directly to the Chairman, and was nevertheless honored without an application in the proceeding or any explanation in the record. This was *ex parte*.

In a political context in which the SEC was only tangentially involved, this telephone call was used more effectively than the facts warranted. Yet it both demonstrates the attitude of Con-

gress and teaches a lesson that independence is deemed sacro-
sanct if the matter before the Commission takes the form of a
quasi-judicial proceeding.

(2) A different question of independence was presented on a
visit which I made to the White House, to obtain support for better quarters for the Securities and Exchange Commission. It
proved to be a good lesson that an agency must rely upon itself.
This was shortly after the stock market break in the spring of
1962. Instead of having the opportunity to broach the subject of
my visit, one of the White House assistants suggested that probably the basic cause of the 1962 market decline was short selling,
and that I should consider bringing this to public attention. He
earnestly believed this was true, and had the notion that it would
help the President politically. I am sure this suggestion had never
been discussed with the President, but I would have had some
difficulty with it had I felt personally beholden to the White
House staff member—if, for example, he had been a sponsor of
my appointment or had supported the agency in budgetary requests. I suggested that his idea would need thorough explora-
tion, and was being given proper attention in our Special Study
of the Securities Markets,[18] but that unless it were thoroughly established I would not accept it myself and could not persuade my
colleagues to go along. Thereupon the assistant called up a colleague and reported that I had said I was chairman of an independent regulatory agency and expected to operate as such. In
this case, at least, the label of independence bore a good result.
The matter was neither judicial nor quasi-judicial, but still involved a commission judgment on a specific issue, rather than a
question of broad policy.

(3) Again the question of subservience might have arisen on
the occasion of a visit by the president of the New York Stock
Exchange to President Johnson in 1964. One of the ostensible reasons for the visit was simply to "get acquainted," since the President had indicated his interest in cooperating with business. Usually, however, persons seeking an appointment have some concrete objective in mind. At that time the main issue between the

---

[18] See *Report of Special Study of the Securities Markets of the SEC*, pt. 2, H.,
p. 246 ff., [hereafter referred to as the *Special Study*].

SEC and the Exchange was an SEC proposal by rule to abolish, or at any rate vastly restrict, the floor trader, who was trading for his personal account on the floor of the Exchange rather than on behalf of public customers. My personal view was that there was no place for private traders on a public market. The issue had become something of a *cause célèbre* in the newspapers at the time. On March 15, 1964, Mr. Funston, the president of the New York Stock Exchange, had attacked the SEC for breaking off negotiations, promised to fight any ban on floor trading, and accused the staff of lack of objectivity.[19] It was widely stated that this was a point on which the New York Stock Exchange was going to seek Presidential support, presumably as a way for him to demonstrate his conciliatory attitude toward business. The fact that the New York Stock Exchange was expected to take up this matter with the President came to the attention of the press. Here was an example of its power, for the visit received such widespread publicity, particularly in the *New York Times*,[20] that Mr. Funston felt compelled to announce beforehand that he was not going to discuss it and, immediately afterwards, that he did not do so in the meeting with the President.[21] As to his visit, there was, in fact, no conversation between anyone in the White House and anyone in the Securities and Exchange Commission either before or afterwards. Still the question is what would have happened if the floor-trading issue had been taken up with the President and he, as a matter of policy, had come to the conclusion that in cooperating with business, this subject should not be aggressively pursued by the Commission. (Inconceivable as it may seem, government action restricting a handful of people from benefiting themselves upon a public marketplace can be magnified, and indeed distorted, by labeling it as an "attack on business.")

Though the matter was in the stage of informal negotiation, prior to rule making and the formal announcement to the pub-

[19] "Big Board Plans Fight to Prevent Floor Trading Ban," Wall Street Journal, March 16, 1964, p. 2, col. 2; "SEC Break with Big Board First in Two Years of Negotiating," N.Y. Times, March 16, 1964, p. 47, col. 8.

[20] "Stock Exchange to Ask Johnson to Intervene in Fight with SEC," N.Y. Times, March 23, 1964, p. 45, cols. 6, 8.

[21] "Funston Confers with Johnson but Avoids Dispute on Trading," N.Y. Times, March 26, 1964, p. 49, col. 2.

lic, in my opinion it would present a very difficult and thorny problem for the White House to express its views to the Commission without endangering its relationship with Congress. Here again, the independence of a commission from the White House may have some reality.

(4) In the case of another agency, while I was in Washington a matter of licensing a damsite as a power facility was pending, in which the Federal Power Commission and a government department were at odds. The suggestion was made that the two groups might meet at the White House to resolve their differences. However, so long as the issue before the Commission took the form of a judicial proceeding, it might have been perilous for the White House to insert itself and possibly to endanger its relations with Congress.

But what if the decision before the agency was whether to prosecute a close case in the courts? The power not to prosecute is one of the most significant ones exercised by a commission. To be concrete, the SEC in 1965 was considering, and finally brought, an action against Texas Gulf Sulphur Company [22] and its directors for trading in its stock after the discovery of a sensational ore strike but before its announcement. The suit had a broad impact in the financial community, and the Commission probably realized that it would. But should the President be consulted? He is charged under Article II, section 3, of the Constitution with responsibility that the laws be faithfully executed. Here again I believe he should not be consulted, though his office might be informed in advance of the press release.

(5) There are cases, however, closer to the border line. After all, commissions are part of government, and the Executive has the constitutional responsibility to see that the laws are enforced. Coordination at the very least should be anticipated. For example, in 1962 Congress authorized a special study of the securities market at a time when the market was high and there were allegations of substantial fraud. This will be discussed in Chapter 3; The Special Study, pages 71 to 79. Even though it had its origin in Congress, clearance of the funds for it had to be through the

---

[22] *SEC v. Texas Gulf Sulphur Company, et al.*, Civil No. 1182/1965, S.D.N.Y., complaint filed April 19, 1965.

18

Bureau of the Budget. But should the approach to be taken in the study be discussed in the White House? Actually, it was not. Yet if it were to be flamboyant, a muckraking investigation that might affect the market, should not there be some coordination with the White House, charged with maintaining our economy in equilibrium? Similarly, insofar as the results might affect the market and thus the economy, I believe that the Commission could not afford to arrive at its final conclusions without giving the White House some advance information as to what they would be. This is what was done.

(6) Let us consider another facet in the relationship between the White House and the Commission at the time of the sudden accession of President Johnson. Upon the death of President Kennedy, his successor made a determined effort to bring us together and instill a renewed sense of purpose and cooperation, in several meetings with the chairmen of the various regulatory agencies. Furthermore, as the time was approaching for the 1964 election, the President not unnaturally was concentrating on the problems of getting reelected, a point of view which President Kennedy or any other realist would undoubtedly have shared. He therefore made the point to the chairmen and others present that this was not the time to rock the boat. He said: [23] "We are challenged [to reevaluate the regulatory roles] . . . to concern ourselves with new areas of cooperation before we concern ourselves with new areas of control. Of course, "rocking the boat" has a different connotation to different people: to some businessmen who do not like to be regulated, it means any action taken to enforce the law. To those of us who entertained the notion that we were simply raising business standards to the level of the high-grade people in the industry, even aggressive action did not seem exceptionable. A definition was never arrived at; but it is likely that the President had certain fundamental legislation in mind to get through Congress and wanted to reduce the number of other variables which might affect his election. Query, then: Should the expression of an attitude on the part of the President, giving the heads of regula-

---

[23] President's Remarks while Meeting with Heads of Independent Regulatory Agencies in Cabinet Room, Dec. 3, 1963, quoted in Redford, *The President and the Regulatory Commissions*, 44 TEXAS L. REV. 288, at 318 (1965).

tory agencies a direction by which to sail, be regarded as improper or subject to congressional criticism? My own view is that it is not improper, although by rationalizing I convinced myself that every action we were proposing to take would not "rock the boat," as he might construe it. I do believe that regulatory agencies are very much a part of the Federal government and affect our economy and American business so importantly that they should be subject to a general framework of national policy, which the President should feel free to express without congressional opposition. If I had been told directly to "slow down," I might have resigned in protest, yet I believe the President should set the general tone which we follow during his administration.

We now come to the breaking point between the views of two experts: Professor Emmette S. Redford [24] and Judge Henry J. Friendly. Mr. Redford believes in the principle of presidential responsibility for coordination and policy development. Referring specifically to his suggestion for policy guides in connection with the FCC, Judge Friendly concluded in his book *The Federal Administrative Agencies*,[25] "Quite simply, I find it hard to think of anything worse."

After three and a half years as a pawn between these two views, I find it impossible to arrive at any absolute formula. If Mr. Redford were in effect seeking to make all the commissions subordinate units of a government department, I should dissent on political, philosophical, and practical grounds. In the first place, it is politically out of the question because Congress still regards them as *its* progeny and agents. For similar reasons, I cannot accept the proposal of a czar in the White House charged with oversight of the agencies, suggested by James M. Landis in his 1960 report. It would be political suicide. As Chairman Oren Harris of the House Interstate and Foreign Commerce Committee has said: [26]

---

[24] For his most recent statement of views, see Redford, cited in footnote directly above.

[25] FRIENDLY, *op. cit.*, p. 153.

[26] Speech Before the United States Chamber of Commerce, Fourth Annual Public Affairs Conference, Washington, D.C., Feb. 4, 1965. Mr. Harris was appointed a judge of the United States District Court in Arkansas in 1965.

Why did these proposals die? Why should their death not be mourned? And, most important of all, is there any occasion for resurrecting them? . . .

        ❋        ❋        ❋

These agencies were created by the Congress in discharging Congress' constitutional responsibilities with regard to the regulation of interstate and foreign commerce. . . . Therefore, Congress traditionally has considered these agencies arms of the Congress. . . .

        ❋        ❋        ❋

With respect to policy development and execution, . . . in the areas under their jurisdiction, Congress sought to avoid executive control, whether such policies were to be developed through rule-making or on a case-by-case basis.

Apparently President Kennedy, who appreciated the delicacy of his own relation with Congress, realized that the Landis suggestion was not politically feasible and therefore, in his message to Congress of April 13, 1961,[27] referring to his "constitutional duty to see that the laws are faithfully executed," said:

> In short, the President's responsibilities require him to know and evaluate how efficiently these agencies dispatch their business, including any lack of prompt decision of the thousands of cases which they are called upon to decide, any failure to evolve policy in areas where they have been charged by the Congress to do so, or any other difficulties that militate against the performance of their statutory duties.

Quite apart from the political impracticality of the suggestion, a czar in the White House would require a person of extraordinarily broad range to provide guidance in more than the most general terms. Who would accept this role? It is not a Cabinet post. It could not be remotely compared with being Secretary of a new Department of Transportation. And yet, unless there is one such person, the White House becomes again a collection of assistants, some of them less competent and experienced than the chair-

---

[27] President Kennedy's Message to the 87th Congress on Regulatory Agencies (April 13, 1961).

men of many of the commissions. Unhappily, in any administration, Democratic or Republican, there seem to be only a select group of assistants of broad talent or experience (in policy as distinguished from tactical matters). The attention of this "first tier" is seldom focused upon the regulatory commissions.

From a philosophical standpoint also, I would favor pluralism within government, power dispersed among a number of independent agencies. Despite their wide impact on business, they are typically administering one or more statutes and a policy which is set by law. Though the policy may be vague, very few of the agency's decisions involve matters which the President himself should, in theory, decide or even be aware of. They would probably fall to the second tier of presidential assistants, who have no guidelines. As Professor Bernstein has pointed out,[28] there is no coherent and coordinated program for national regulation of economic affairs. Thus, the alternative is to retain the independent commissions, with full recognition that they are not wholly divorced from the political tensions generated by both Congress and the White House. It is true that there are other agencies performing a comparable regulatory role but included as a subordinate unit within one of the government Departments. Perhaps some of them might also be given independent status, but they must be sufficiently important not to get lost, to merit separate oversight by Congress and the White House.

But, one may ask, can we base a system on decision making by the President on the one hand and presidential assistants on the other? What if the President himself had asked the agency not to prosecute an action? The answer is not affected. The system should not depend on who makes the particular decision, but on whether the decisions of the agency are so crucial that the President should pass upon them. If they are not, then "independence" should be preserved. It is likely to ensure more freedom from "politics" in its less favorable sense.

Finally, as a practical matter, if the agencies were subordinated, they would probably fit under the Department of Commerce, already a hodgepodge of undistinguished bureaus princi-

[28] BERNSTEIN, *op. cit.*, p. 163.

pally aimed at promoting business rather than regulating it. They would have little hope of vitality or even occasional revitalization under Commerce Department aegis.

* * *

We have already discussed a series of actual situations which occurred during the Kennedy and Johnson regimes. Perhaps two hypothetical ones may provide further guidance. First of all, when I took office in 1961 the market was turbulent and new issues of securities were at an all-time high. Not only were there more registration statements, but 60 percent of them involved securities of new companies which had never before been offered to the public. The SEC was not equipped with enough experienced manpower to handle them, so we had to take personal responsibility for less careful processing of the materials.[29] If we had failed to take this responsibility, there might have been a log jam in the capital market, which would have affected the economy. In such a situation I assume that the White House could exercise authority, because we would have been derelict in our duty. This would be a case of inefficiency. White House participation here would be in accord with President Kennedy's own statement and in my opinion would even be acceptable to Congress.

Second, let us consider the decision of the Federal Communications Commission in late 1965 to make a formal investigation into the rate structure of the American Telephone & Telegraph Company.[30] There had been no such investigation since the thirties; rate reductions had been achieved exclusively through informal negotiations. This announcement was made at a time when President Johnson, generally attempting to maintain a consensual relationship with business, was being criticized for the first time by reason of action he took as to price rises in certain key industries, notably steel and aluminum. Let us therefore assume that he is not anxious to become more embroiled than is necessary. He does not want to be accused of attacking business. If we move back four years, we would have had the same question during the re-

---

[29] See generally SEC Ann. Rep., 28, p. 4 (1962).
[30] N.Y. Times, Oct. 28, 1965, p. 1, col. 1; see also Dec. 24, 1964, p. 27, col. 1.

gime of President Kennedy after his confrontation with the steel industry, but on a more dramatic scale because it was alleged to have contributed to a recession.

The implications of the AT&T investigation may be considered by the public to be broader than they actually are. In the first place, it may be regarded as action against business sponsored by the President or at least having his blessing. Although limited to a single company, in effect it is directed at the entire telephone industry. In the second place, the investigation had the possibility of affecting the price of AT&T common shares; in fact a decline in the market price took place in January of 1966, which led an FCC spokesman to express concern and regret that its action had been misinterpreted.[31] On these hypotheses the issues are drawn: first of all, should the White House be informed of the action proposed to be taken; second, should the advice of the President be sought; third, should he feel free to make known his views as to whether or not an investigation should be instituted at this time?

In my opinion the President should be informed of the decision that has been reached before it is announced—just as he was informed in advance of the content of our Special Study—but his advice should not be sought. If, on the other hand, the President wishes to state his views, either that he thinks the investigation is wrongly timed or wrongly conceived, I think it should be proper for him to do so. He can make a public statement, or have the Council of Economic Advisers speak on his behalf. I do not think that his discouragement of the project should bind the commission. Realistically he can hamstring the investigation through the budget and through refusal to provide any more supergrades to bring in competent persons to handle the investigation. And if the investigation were conducted irresponsibly and began to have some repercussions in the market, he could remove the chairman and appoint another from the commission membership.

Conversely, if the President had appointed a new FCC chairman on the assumption that he would be vigorous and found him complacent rather than willing to undertake such an investigation, he has the power to choose another. He might even appoint

---

[31] "A.T. & T. Decline Worrying F.C.C.", N.Y. Times, Feb. 3, 1966, p. 41, col. 4.

a committee outside the FCC to make a study of the future problems arising from developments in the industry. He should also have the right, indeed the duty, to say that the agency is not performing vigorously and up to his expectations.

At the same time, I share the views of Professor Clark Byse [32] and Professor Carl McFarland.[33] They do not believe the regulatory agencies should be free from executive control on matters of broad policy, particularly if the policy issue affects more than one agency or if it is an issue which the Executive Office believes is of critical national importance. But relatively few issues before the independent commissions are of such magnitude. The decisions of these agencies are in no way comparable to those of the Federal Reserve Board in their economic or political significance. I would amplify my position by insisting that presidential policy be open. It need not always be publicly stated, but it should be a policy position which the White House should be prepared to publish if the occasion arises. The basic objection to executive control arises from the fact that it may be undercover and therefore "political" in the unsavory way.

There are further reasons why I do not feel that doctrinaire, total "independence" from the White House should be insisted upon. While we were in Washington a small group of agency heads used to meet informally once a month, originally at the suggestion of Newton Minow, FCC chairman, and Najeeb Halaby, Administrator of the Federal Aviation Administration. One of the objectives was to achieve some coordination, particularly among the transportation agencies, and another to compare experiences. Appropriately enough, we called ourselves "The Tightrope Club." We were cautious about meeting with the White House or making public our existence, in part because of congressional reaction. I believe this is unfortunate. Perhaps the trouble lies in the attitude that Congress has toward the independent regulatory agency: that it is a judicial, or at least quasi-judicial, body. But policy is developed through rule making—legislation—and deci-

---

[32] Byse, *Proposals for Administrative Agencies*, 32 HARV. LAW RECORD (No. 1), p. 9 (1961).

[33] McFarland, *Landis' Report: The Voice of One Crying in the Wilderness*, 47 VA. L. REV. 373, at 438 (1961).

sions to bring action or, equally important, not to bring action. Adjudication is only one avenue and should not be overemphasized, by Congress or otherwise.

The second attitude of Congress, already repeated many times, is that the commissions are exclusively arms of Congress. Congress should abandon this cliché and acknowledge that the White House has, and indeed already exercises, a role through the appointment power, budget, and its authority over legislation and elsewhere. The House Subcommittee on Legislative Oversight said, in its concluding report: [34]

Effective reform of the administrative process requires teamwork between the Executive and Congress. In a time when united national effort is needed more than ever before in our history to improve the efficiency of our constitutional system of government, it would be tragic to have a conflict develop between the Executive and Congress over the question of which branch has supreme control over the Federal agencies.

Congress might do well to heed its own advice.

---

[34] H.R. REP. 2238, 86th Cong., 2d Sess., p. 43 (1961).

# 2 | *The Congress*

## *Attitude toward Regulatory Agencies*

*Reorganization Plan No. 1 of 1961.* The jealous attitude of Congress has already been indicated in the colloquy in the Senate over Sherman Adams' telephone call. Senators and representatives stress "independence," but only *from* the White House. A commission is an agent of Congress. During my own period in Washington the temper of Congress can be further illustrated by its position in connection with the reorganization plans of 1961.[1] Five of them were filed: the first involving the SEC;[2] the second, the FCC; the third, the CAB; the fourth, the FTC; and the fifth, the NLRB. The thesis underlying all of them can be said to have been spawned by Mr. Landis in his Report on Regulatory Agencies of December 21, 1960. Two of his criticisms involved the delay in the disposition of adjudication proceedings and the neglect by the commissions of their planning or creative functions.[3] He suggested more delegation of responsibility to the staff, and also formal acknowledgment of existing *de facto* delegation. As he put

---

[1] See generally *The Progress of Federal Agency Reorganization under the Kennedy Administration,* 48 VA. L. REV. 300 (1962).

[2] Transmitted to the Senate and the House, April 27, 1961. See H.R. DOC. No. 146, 87th Cong., 1st Sess. (1961).

[3] *Landis Report,* pp. 5 and 22.

27

it,[4] "The real issue that we face is whether to recognize openly this fact of delegation or continue with the present facade of non-delegation, which prevents administrators from doing the work for which they have been appointed." In the final recommendations of his report, therefore, he proposed a reorganization plan for the seven major independent regulatory agencies providing for the delegation of all adjudicatory matters, subject only to discretionary review by the agency on petition by a party in interest.

Mr. Landis' report was a helpful document. Written by the former chairman of two different agencies, it did not purport to provide all the solutions but pointed to many of the weaknesses of regulatory agencies. Furthermore, a proposal such as delegation seemed basically sound, if it were properly handled with Congress. Thus the major difficulty lay in the mode of its submission rather than in the merits of the plan itself. It may be said to have been soundly conceived but ineptly executed. Perhaps the trouble lay in submitting the program to Congress under authority of the Reorganization Act of 1949 (as amended).[5] It provides that a reorganization plan will become effective sixty days after its submission to Congress unless either house has passed a resolution disapproving it within that time. However sound it may be, the submission of a reorganization plan almost by definition seems to meet with congressional suspicion. I have heard Chairman Oren Harris suggest that a program which I once had in mind (See Chapter 3; The Special Study, page 70.)—to divest the SEC of jurisdiction over utility holding companies—might be entertained by the House in the form of a bill but never as a plan.

Quite apart from congressional malaise with reorganization plans as such, there was at the time a feeling of distrust about the motives in the White House. The newspapers had made much of the fact that Mr. Landis was located in the Executive Office of the White House and would be acting as "czar" of the regulatory agencies. So far as I know there was no truth to this beyond the recommendations in his report, but there need be none to make the political problem exist.

[4] *Landis Report*, p. 20.
[5] 5 U.S.C. § 133(z) (1964).

Finally, as a matter of political strategy, it is an unhappy fact that the chairmen of the SEC, FCC, and CAB, the first three agencies subject to reorganization, were informed by the White House just a few days in advance that the plans were to be submitted to Congress immediately. Our views were (in effect) canvased almost overnight. Most of us had just taken office and were just getting acquainted with our fellow commissioners, and further we were not clear whether formal powers of delegation were needed. At the time, my initial reaction was that we already had adequate powers to delegate and hence did not need further statutory authorization, but in retrospect I may have been wrong. Yet the facts are that none of us had an opportunity to comment effectively as to our own agency on a reorganization plan which was to be uniformly overlaid upon us all. Having taken office on March 27, 1961, I had to appear before the House on Reorganization Plan No. 1 on May 18. Happily, it passed the House. Before the Senate Committee on Government Operations on June 6, the immediate question was asked me by the chairman, Senator McClellan, as follows: [6]

THE CHAIRMAN. You spoke about the real issue—being fair and reasonable in your decision—and then raised some question there as to whether you would in the delegation of authority be reasonable. I think the concern is this, and I share it to some extent, that we want to keep these boards or commissions independent. Nobody wants them to get under the domination of the President, or the assistant to the President, or somebody else. We want to keep them independent, where they exercise a judgment and a judicial function of their own, influenced by the merits and by the record, and not one that comes under the executive branch of the Government as such. That is a question that has been raised.

Is there anything in this that you feel would to any degree diminish the present independent status of the commission, or in any degree threaten that independence and freedom of judgment as it has been heretofore exercised?

In answer to this question, I felt in a position to assure the Senator that our independence would not be threatened and that in-

___

[6] *Hearings Before the Senate Committee on Government Operations,* 87th Cong., 1st Sess. [Reorganization Plans of 1961] (June 6, 1961), at 51.

deed I could take no action as chairman without the concurrence of my fellow commissioners. This represented one of the concerns of the Senate.

The FCC testified on the same day in connection with Reorganization Plan No. 2, but was not able to speak effectively as a commission. The Associate General Counsel of the FCC appeared before the Senate committee representing the chairman and two other commissioners who supported the reorganization plan, and the Assistant General Counsel appeared representing the other four commissioners who did not.[7] This posed a problem far more embarrassing to the FCC than to the SEC.

Since the proposal was an Administration plan which had been handed to us as soon as we arrived, without benefit of our comment, and since most of us did not know our way around Congress at the beginning, perhaps we should have anticipated trouble over its passage. The New York Stock Exchange strongly opposed our plan and had the backing of Senator Javits (Republican, New York). I myself was undoubtedly naïve in expecting it to pass the Senate. But the first news I heard of its defeat [8] was a call from Senator Javits, who said that it had just been disapproved. He then added that he and Senator Williams (Democrat, New Jersey), as two of the Republican and Democratic leaders of the Banking and Currency Committee having jurisdiction over the SEC, had already agreed to sponsor a bill giving us most of the authority which would have been available under the reorganization plan.[9]

The FCC plan was also defeated, although Plan No. 3 involving the CAB got by with a thin margin.[10] Under any circumstances, the vote had given the Senate (and not exclusively the Republican minority) the opportunity to advise the President of its own power and of the limitations upon the executive power. The White House was of course upset, and one of the assistants

---

[7] *Id.* at 57.

[8] 107 CONG. REC. 11003 (1961).

[9] S. 2135, 87th Cong., 1st Sess.; see 107 CONG. REC. 11032 (1961).

[10] Plan No. 3 became law on July 3, 1961, the date on which the time limit expired. 26 FED. REG. 5989 (1961). The House vote is recorded at 107 CONG. REC. 10844 (1961), and the Senate vote at 107 CONG. REC. 11748 (1961).

called to criticize us, but he received few apologies. At the time, the Chairman of the FCC told the White House emphatically that he would get a bill through that he wanted without their participation, and I was inclined to feel the same way. There was nothing wrong with the plan in substance; in my opinion the real problem lay in how it was drafted and presented. This is one of the earliest examples of the difficulty encountered by the Kennedy administration in piloting legislation through Congress.

Ultimately both the SEC [11] and the FCC succeeded in having bills passed which gave the agencies broad power to delegate their functions to commission personnel below the level of a full commissioner. Senate Bill 2135 involving the SEC granted this power in much the same fashion as Reorganization Plan No. 1 of 1961, but with certain variations designed to meet the principal objections. The differences from Reorganization Plan No. 1 lay in two areas: (1) the circumstances under which the full Commission would be required to review action taken at a delegated level; and (2) the authority of the Commission to delegate the function of rule making. As to the latter point particularly, in order to head off opposition to Plan 1 before the Senate and also to carry out our initial intent, we carefully stated that we did not plan to delegate any of the agency's major rule making functions. Yet frequently Congress is not satisfied with a statement in the record but insists upon spelling it out into the statute. Therefore Senate 2135 explicitly prohibits delegation of any rule making within the broad definition of the Administrative Procedure Act.

*The Impasse in the ICC.* Another demonstration of the attitude of Congress toward the regulatory commissions lies in the story of the ICC. There was a time when this Commission assumed a wider responsibility in the transportation field. Its outstanding members like Joseph B. Eastman did not limit their sights to assuring reasonable rates and absence of discrimination.[12] However, during the decade of the fifties and—while it has been showing some signs of life—even until the present, the agency

---

[11] S. 2135 became law. Pub. L. No. 592, 87th Cong., 1st Sess. (Aug. 20, 1962).
[12] See BERNSTEIN, pp. 50–52; see generally LATHAM, THE POLITICS OF RAILROAD COORDINATION 1933–1936 (Harv. Univ. Press 1959).

has been notoriously moribund and overjudicialized. Mr. Landis in his report late in 1960 indicated that the ICC was among the agencies principally calling for reorganization. He said (p. 37): [13]

It lacks positive direction because of the absence of the position of a chairman who is other than a presiding officer. The theory of a rotating chairman, elected annually by the membership, may assuage the ambitions of its membership, but it deprives the commission of that leadership that it so sadly needs. . . . It is . . . essential that he be appointed to that office by the President and hold it at his pleasure.

In addition, Mr. Landis concluded that the membership of the Commission, eleven in number and the largest of any regulatory agency, gave ground for concern, and concluded further that the "opinions of the Interstate Commerce Commission are presently in the poorest category of all administrative agency opinions." [14] He felt that a major problem in the reorganization of the ICC was the delegation of appropriate duties to persons below the commission level.

Among all the so-called independent regulatory agencies, the ICC probably enjoys the most independence. This seems to be what Congress wants; at least, it has been reluctant to accept any structural change. President Truman failed in his effort to reorganize the Commission under Plan No. 7 of 1950.[15] The reasons for this independence date back at least to 1935, to the strongly held views of Commissioner Eastman. At a meeting of the National Emergency Council in December, 1935, at which President Roosevelt was present, Mr. Eastman opposed prior clearance of testimony of ICC commissioners before Congress and engaged in the following colloquy: [16]

MR. EASTMAN. I am sure it is not the intention to apply that policy to the independent agencies, such as the Interstate Commerce Commission. That is the servant of Congress and is directed by law

[13] *Landis Report,* p. 37.
[14] *Landis Report,* p. 39.
[15] *Landis Report,* p. 36.
[16] BERNSTEIN, p. 63.

to make reports to Congress. The report of the Interstate Commerce Commission does not go to the President. It goes to Congress, and it is in the habit of committees of Congress to ask our opinion on almost every bill that comes up.

PRESIDENT ROOSEVELT. But, again, there you forget that the Constitution provides that the President is head of the Executive branch of the Government. Congress cannot set up the Interstate Commerce Commission as a separate agency and not in any way related to the President. Therefore, the Interstate Commerce Commission I think would be on the wise side if, when asked for an opinion on a matter of policy, they would consult the President.

MR. EASTMAN. Of course there is a question whether the Interstate Commerce Commission is a member of the Executive branch. Its work is largely legislative, established by law. I have served not only in a Democratic Administration, but in a Republican as well. I know it has certain judicial functions.

There have been continuing arguments over the independence of the ICC since 1935. One of the issues still is whether or not the ICC must submit its annual report and proposed legislation to the Bureau of the Budget. Neither seems to be required.

Unfortunately, independence has not generated policy planning nor an imaginative agency program. Most of the cases on its docket do not bear on the public interest. One of the ICC commissioners said to me that the advantage of rotating chairmen was continuity; but this very continuity seems to have made impossible any movement ahead. It might better be described as circular. The ICC needs a new charter and a paring of functions. Furthermore, in any agency with so many commissioners, the tendency to judicialize its actions is inevitable.

Despite the views of Mr. Landis, which to my knowledge were shared by most of the principal advisers of President Kennedy, there was no reorganization plan filed with respect to the ICC nor any formal proposal for an appointed chairman in lieu of a rotating one. Internally, after the Landis Report there was probably more action by the agency itself than at any time in fifteen years in reconstituting its own procedures. However, in the White House the ICC was recognized as being so politically sensitive that any effort toward a drastic reorganization would bring congressional pressures and jealousy into play.

It is too narrow to attribute the plight of the ICC to the Commission alone, although it has demonstrated little initiative in extricating itself. The deeper problem lies in the politics of transportation and the vested interests which have found congressional support. There is opposition from all sides to the obvious need for coordination. An illustration of the difficulty of any movement forward lies in the fate of the transportation bill, sponsored by the Kennedy and Johnson administrations, opposed by the ICC, and ultimately killed in the Rules Committee by a very slight margin.[17] As a general proposition, it can be said that the railroads today are seeking less regulation, while the truckers and water carriers are seeking more in order to discourage competition. To some extent, a reduction in regulation was the object of the transportation bill, which met opposition from trucking concerns and water carriers. Even with the support of the committee chairman, in view of the pressures and counterpressures within the transportation industry it was impossible to have a bill passed. They account in considerable part for the ultimate defeat of any effort to change the transportation situation.

In this political context the suggestions of Mr. Landis in his report seem unduly optimistic. His notion,[18] for example, of having an overall transportation czar within the Executive Office of the President has much to be said for it in theory but would accentuate existing political antagonisms. Congress favors the *status quo*. It is perhaps too much, therefore, to expect more than halting steps in improving transportation. One step was taken in 1965 in placing an experienced man as Undersecretary of Commerce for Transportation, i.e., the former chairman of the Civil Aeronautics Board. Now in 1966 the President has proposed a Department of Transportation, but his Message on Transportation [19] carefully limited its role and said the cabinet-level Department "would

---

[17] See *Transportation Amendments of 1964,* H.R. Rep. 1144, 88th Cong., 2d Sess. (Feb. 18, 1964).

[18] *Landis Report,* p. 77.

[19] President Johnson's Message on Transportation bears the date of March 1, 1966.

not alter the economic regulatory functions of the ICC, the CAB, or the Federal Maritime Commission." Borrowing from the Landis report, the Presidential message recognized that it is utterly impossible to achieve any real resuscitation of an agency with an annually rotating chairman. Unfortunately it did not adopt a further Landis recommendation, i.e., that the size of the Commission must be cut. The message read in part:

> Today, the chairman of this vital commission—alone among the federal regulatory agencies—is selected, not by the president, but by annual rotation among the eleven commissioners.
>
> This is not sound management practice in an agency whose influence on our rail, highway, waterway and pipeline industries is so far-reaching.
>
> The I.C.C. bears the demanding and challenging responsibility to keep federal regulation attuned to the needs and opportunities of a dynamic industry. Its jurisdiction extends to 18,000 transport companies. It handles 7,000 cases each year. No private corporation of such size and importance would change its chief executive officer each year.
>
> *I shall shortly submit to the Congress a reorganization plan to give the President authority to designate the chairman of the Interstate Commerce Commission from among its members, and to strengthen his executive functions.*

But can Congress be persuaded? Does it really want impotency?

### Direct Congressional Power over Agencies

*The Budget.* The foregoing examples illustrate the general attitude of Congress toward the regulatory agencies, and particularly a distrust of the White House. The relationship may be further described by identifying the direct powers which Congress exercises over the "independent" commissions. Congressional power, of course, is generally exercised through committees. Specifically, budgetary matters are handled by the Committee on Appropriations in both the House and the Senate, and in most instances the substantive work of the six commissions is subject to the jurisdiction of the Interstate and Foreign Commerce Committee of the

House and its counterpart in the Senate. For purely historical reasons, however, the Securities and Exchange Commission looks to the Banking and Currency Committee of the Senate.

Congress has been more than willing to exercise its budgetary authority over the activities of regulatory commissions during the Kennedy and Johnson administrations. Indeed, that is one reason why any chairman of an agency must spend a very substantial part of his time on Capitol Hill. In my own case, our subcommittee chairman, the late Albert Thomas, made the remark, "I recall the first year Mr. Cary was here I thought he was in the office with us over here all the time. . . ." [20]

As earlier noted, until the beginning of 1960 it is fair to say that all the regulatory agencies had been starved for funds. The point was made concretely by a predecessor, J. Sinclair Armstrong. In the context of legislative oversight, he pointed out Congress' consistent refusal to recognize the Commission's budget requirements. From 1940 to 1954 it had cut the staff from 1800 to 700 with frequent support from the Bureau of the Budget. In 1957 he was placed in a most difficult position when appearing before a subcommittee of the Committee on Banking and Currency of the Senate in support of legislation to expand certain investor protections to all companies having wide public stock ownership, the precursor of the Securities Acts Amendments of 1964. He was asked: "Do you think it would be worth $500,000 to bring all of these companies in?" And the colloquy continued as follows: [21]

MR. ARMSTRONG. I believe that it would be very desirable for legislation of this character to be passed, but we are in such a very difficult situation in regard to staffing our Commission at the present time that I just cannot say whether it would be worth $500,000. Very frankly, the House committee took away from us $478,000 in the 1958 appropriation, and it is a very, very serious thing. They directed that the increase they did give us should not be used in the Washington office. Now, the Division of Corporation

---

[20] *Hearings Before a Subcommittee of the House Committee on Appropriations for Fiscal Year 1964,* 88th Cong., 1st Sess. (Jan. 31, 1963), p. 515.
[21] *Hearings Before a Subcommittee of the Senate Committee on Banking and Currency,* 85th Cong., 1st Sess. [SEC Legislation] (May 20–29, 1957), p. 66.

Finance that Mr. Woodside administers down here costs us about $1,200,000 to administer. We are examining twice as many registration statements per month as we were in 1953. The volume of work has doubled, and we have less staff than we had in 1953. We have got 65 percent of the staff the Commission had 10 years ago.

The blame, however, should not be fastened on one branch of government. It must be borne in part by the Budget Bureau (acting on behalf of the White House). Mr. Landis said in his report.[22]

The agency heads themselves, presumably under the general direction of the Executive Office of the President, curtailed their requests despite the growing pressure of the business pending before them for disposition. Congress similarly exhibited the same tendencies.

With the advent of the Kennedy administration, a spirit of change began to prevail and seemed to be shared by Congress. Prior to that time the commissions not only had been starved but had not been in good repute because of several scandals. Perhaps, realistically, one of the main reasons for the shift in attitude was that the committee chairmen and the President were now of the same party. Nevertheless, during the succeeding years, to illustrate, the budget of the SEC moved from $9,517,000 and 1,090 employees for the fiscal year (ending June 30) 1960 to $13,937,500 and 1,468 employees in fiscal 1964.[23] Most of the independent regulatory agencies received comparable increases.

At the same time, the Appropriations Committee was not entirely willing to provide a carte blanche to the agencies. The Chairman of the Federal Power Commission, for example, regulating gas rates, might be expected to have some special problems with the subcommittee chairman, who represented a constituency in Texas. In the 1964 report of the House Appropriations Committee the comment was made that

The Federal Power Commission is an important agency, but it has grown almost 40 percent in jobs since 1960. Along with growth in

---

[22] *Landis Report,* p. 7.
[23] SEC ANN. REP. 31, for Fiscal Year 1965, p. 157.

jobs there is much complaint that the Agency is foot-dragging in its disposal of cases. The Committee urges the Commission to cut down its delay in disposing of cases as it is hurting the industries it has to regulate. . . . The Commission is spending too much time in empire building and trying to expand its jurisdiction.[24]

Here there was a basic difference in point of view on the substantive question of fixing rates for natural gas at the wellhead.

Appropriations committees tend to go even further in instructing the agencies specifically how their funds should be spent. To illustrate with respect to the Federal Trade Commission, the House committee report on Independent Offices Appropriations for 1964 states [25] that "The $100,000 included in the 1964 budget program for a general questionnaire and economic study of intercorporate relations has been denied and a limitation has been included in the bill prohibiting the use of funds for this purpose." In the Independent Offices Appropriations for 1965 the report states that the same limitation is carried over into the bill again for another year.

Again the attitude of the Senate Appropriations Committee toward the Federal Power Commission can be illustrated from the following quotation in the report for 1965: [26]

> In its report on the 1964 independent offices appropriations bill, the committee specified that no funds be spent by the FPC to establish regulatory authority over REA cooperatives until the Congress had an opportunity to consider pending legislation clarifying the intent of Congress on this subject. The Commission disregarded the committee's wishes and expended considerable sums of money in a proceeding. . . . Therefore, the committee repeats that no funds should be [so] used . . . until the Congress has had ample opportunity to consider the question. The committee hopes that the Commission will not choose to defy its wishes again this year.

---

[24] House Appropriations Committee, *Report on Independent Offices Appropriation Bill, 1964,* H.R. REP. No. 824, 88th Cong., 1st Sess. (Oct. 7, 1963), p. 9.
[25] *Ibid.*
[26] Senate Appropriations Committee, *Report on Independent Offices Appropriation Bill, 1965,* S. REP. No. 269, 88th Cong., 2d Sess. (July 30, 1964), p. 8.

Control by the Appropriations Committee over substantive programs is well illustrated as to the SEC during the year 1963. Our Commission had taken the position that the Securities Act of 1933 and the Investment Company Act of 1940 were applicable to the offering of public participations in so-called commingled funds operated by banks. In sum, we said that banks offering interests in a pooled investment were selling mutual funds, and their distribution fell within the jurisdiction of the SEC. The policy question was controversial and the Comptroller of the Currency had opposed us (see Chapter 4; Obstacles in the House, page 100).

When we appeared before the Senate Committee on Appropriations, a question on this substantive issue was raised. After extended interrogation it became clear that several senators were antagonistic, and they later succeeded in having inserted in the part of the Committee report relating to the SEC the following restrictive language: [27]

The committee notes the conflict of asserted jurisdiction in the field of administration of common trust funds. It is our opinion that national banks are adequately supervised by the Comptroller of the Currency, and directs [sic] that no funds appropriated in this bill be expended by the SEC for that purpose.

When this restriction by the Appropriations Committee was brought to the attention of Chairman Robertson of the Banking and Currency Committee, who was also a member of the Committee on Appropriations, he raised the issue on the Senate floor as follows: [28]

MR. ROBERTSON. Today for the first time, I find that during my absence the Appropriations Committee took jurisdiction away from our committee and inserted, in the committee report on the pending bill, language which would exempt, or which would try to exempt, the banks from this regulation. But they cannot exempt them from

[27] Senate Committee on Appropriations, *Report on Independent Offices Appropriation Bill, 1964*, S. Rep. No. 641, 88th Cong., 1st Sess. (Nov. 13, 1963), p. 21.
[28] 109 Cong. Rec. 22427–22428 (1963).

the criminal provisions or from possible liability to third persons for violation of the act. Some banker may be mislead [*sic*] into doing things which would put him in jail by taking from the committee that handles the bill jurisdiction over the subject, by writing that language into the committee report. It is just that simple. . . .

MR. MAGNUSON. The language in the report is intended to do the reverse of what is suggested by the Senator from Virginia. It is not intended to take jurisdiction away from the Senator's committee, but to hold this matter in abeyance, when there is a conflict and a controversy as to who has jurisdiction, until the committee can make a decision. . . .

MR. ROBERTSON. A Member of the Senate introduced a bill to take the banks out from under the Investment Company Act. The Banking and Currency Committee has not gotten around to the point of acting on that bill, so now somebody from the Appropriations Committee steps in to say, "No money under the bill can be spent to enforce the law."

MR. MAGNUSON. Oh, no; that is not a proper interpretation. . . .

Senator Anderson also expressed his displeasure at this technique on the Senate floor, describing it as "a new method of putting legislation into an appropriation bill in such fashion that it cannot be attacked by either House." In response to Senator Magnuson's statement that the agency could ignore what the committee says in its report, Senator Anderson said,[29] "But the agency would have its head chopped off when its representatives appeared before the Appropriations Committee at the next session. . . ."

The jurisdiction, therefore, of the Senate and House appropriations committees not only includes fixing the amount of funds allocable to each of the agencies, but also may be stretched to cover the specific purposes for which those funds should be used. Certainly in theory this is a development which should not be permitted to grow. It is an interference with the prerogatives of the substantive committee. As a "bureaucrat" I resisted it to the utmost. Yet when one realizes the numerous agencies and depart-

[29] 109 CONG. REC. 22359 (1963).

ments which any one committee is charged with overseeing, there is some logic in favoring multiple supervision. Furthermore, the details of administration of statutes written in broad language seem to come before appropriations committees. Can Congress really exercise detailed supervision except in the course of the process of appropriating? It is clear that this committee maintains the most systematic and continuous examination of an agency's activities.

*Substantive Aspects.* The power exercised over regulatory agencies by substantive committees of Congress is both broader and usually more channeled than that exercised by the Appropriations Committee in shaping the budget. The dependence, indeed the subservience, of an agency to a committee chairman of the House and Senate, will be treated in Chapter 4: "Shepherding an Agency-sponsored Bill through Congress." Quite apart from the pressures when a commission is trying to obtain legislation, there are other possible ways by which Congress can express its attitude toward an agency's program.

OVERSIGHT. If its reaction is one of marked antagonism, a congressional investigation or simply hearings by a legislative oversight committee can so paralyze an agency that it is incapable of taking any steps forward and at best can only meet its immediate commitments. The layer of top quality experienced personnel in any commission is thin, and must be fully deployed when it is under congressional scrutiny. Yet oversight is an indispensable element in maintaining some control over government action. Sometimes it is salutary, and at other times a source of frustration. The latter was illustrated in the case of a predecessor, J. Sinclair Armstrong, in his article entitled "Congress and the Securities and Exchange Commission": [30]

[I]n the winter of 1957 Speaker Sam Rayburn . . . launched a full-fledged investigation of the independent regulatory agencies "to see whether or not the law as we intended it is being carried out or whether a great many of these laws are being repealed or revamped by those who administer them."

---

[30] 45 VA. L. REV. 795, at 810–811, 816 (1959).

Thus began the fantastic performance of the Subcommittee on Legislative Oversight. Again the Commission was called upon to furnish untold reports, questionnaire answers, personnel and space for Subcommittee personnel. The Commission cooperated with the Subcommittee in every possible way, devoting approximately 10,000 man hours to the inquiry. Statutory inadequacies, the Commission's conduct in particular cases, its administrative policies, its relationships with other agencies and offices in the executive branch and with Congress were gone into.

About the only subject touched constructively was the problem of Congress' consistent refusals to recognize realistically the Commission's budget requirements. From 1940 to 1954 Congress had reduced the Commission's staff, by successive budget cuts, from about 1,800 to less than 700.

* * *

Representative Oren Harris, Chairman of the House Interstate and Foreign Commerce Committee, aghast at the $475,000 cut attempted by the House in the President's recommended SEC budget for 1960, acknowledged that his criticisms of the Commission's actions could all be traced to its staff stringency. Surely for this failure in recent years Congress can blame no one but itself.

* * *

It is high time that Congress resumed its constitutional responsibilities as a legislature and considered the Commission's legislative needs, instead of trying to be a 537-man board of directors overseeing the executive functions of the agency.

Professor Carl MacFarland characterized the performance somewhat differently. He said,[31] "[The] new committee on 'Legislative Oversight' unexpectedly lived up to its odd title. It immediately became involved in an imbroglio over an exposé of questionable conduct of federal commissioners, overlooking the more prosaic —and much more important—problem of simple nonfeasance."

Experience varies in each administration as to Congress' exercise of its responsibilities for oversight. It is difficult enough for an agency which I have described as a stepchild, but it is even

_____
[31] McFarland, *Landis Report: The Voice of One Crying in the Wilderness,* 47 VA. L. REV. 373, at 376 (1961).

more difficult when the stepparents are divorced (the President being of one party and the Congress controlled by another). In my era, luckily, the atmosphere had changed markedly. One had always to be watchful, but the oversight on the part of the House committee and its staff proved helpful. Sometimes we were pressed into positions we were reluctant to take, but properly so. For example, the subcommittee chairman, Mr. Staggers,[32] asked this crucial question:

> With the termination of these hearings on this legislation I should like to conclude by asking you just one question. . . .
> The question is simply this. If this bill is considered favorably by the committee and enacted by the Congress, with any amendments that we might put into it, will you then have the tools which you think are adequate for the protection of the American investment public?
> I want no slip-up on this. You have indicated in your previous appearance time and time again that the Commission is not lacking power in the rulemaking field to do most of the things that are necessary to protect the American investor. So I ask you again, with this bill, will you have the tools that you need to give adequate protection to the American investment public?

The reply was:

> Mr. Chairman, I would say we do. In other words, we don't promise to do a perfect job, but we will do the best job we know how and think we would have the powers.

OVERSIGHT AND SELF-REGULATION. To some extent congressional supervision was also helpful to the SEC in exercising its responsibility, in turn, over the exchanges (with respect to listed securities) and the National Association of Securities Dealers (with respect to the over-the-counter market). Self-regulation is a unique feature of the securities industry, far exceeding in importance the role of the National Association of Broadcasters in the case of ra-

---

[32] *House Hearings* [pt. 2, Investor Protection], (Feb. 19, 1964), p. 1356; Reprinted in H.R. REP. No. 1418, 88th Cong., 2d Sess. (May 19, 1964), pp. 6–7.

dio and television. It rests upon two premises: first, it provides an alternative to more pervasive direct control by government, which would be expensive to the taxpayers and burdensome to the industry; second, it is a more sensitive and effective means of reaching unethical as distinct from illegal conduct. Self-regulation does not mean total autonomy, but rather independence somewhat in the same relative sense as the SEC is said to be independent of Congress.[33] Quite properly, in an industry dealing with securities oversight is called for. And with the profit motive at the root of our economic system, regulation of the industry in the interest of the public cannot be left exclusively to the practitioners, public-spirited as they may be. Furthermore, any institution, whether a Federal commission or a quasi-public institution like an exchange or the NASD, can suffer loss of purpose in the absence of outside criticism.

Oversight on the part of the SEC can benefit an exchange just as congressional oversight can benefit the Commission. The New York Stock Exchange provides an illustration: despite its prestige it is sensitive to criticism. In 1961, its president had objected strongly to my description of it as "having certain characteristics of a private club—a very good one, I might say." [34] It was in this context that the Commission and the New York Stock Exchange in 1964 came into direct conflict [35]—specifically over the continuance of floor traders, already mentioned in Chapter 1; Degrees of Dependence on, and Independence from, the White House, page 17. Here were men trading for their own account exclusively, upon a public market. They reflected a vestigial remnant of the club. Under these circumstances, I was strongly of the opinion that floor traders should be abolished. A confrontation with the Exchange resulted in a compromise, pursuant to which their number was reduced from 300-odd to roughly 30.

Another aspect of the private club was the domination of the Exchange by insiders. We took the position that the governing board of the New York Stock Exchange should not depend exclu-

[33] See *Cary, Self-regulation in the Securities Industry,* 49 A.B.A. J. 244 (1963).
[34] See N.Y. Times, March 16, 1964, p. 47, col. 8.
[35] See N.Y. Times, March 23, 1964, p. 45, cols. 6, 8; March 26, 1964, p. 49, col. 2.

sively on the number of seats owned by its members: there should be stronger representation from the member firms that dealt with the public and generated all the business, i.e., the large national wire houses, and less control in the hands of the floor members.* This too was resisted. Yet the Exchange found it difficult to answer the question why it levied such a high proportion of charges against the public firms to build an insurance reserve (and to meet the liabilities of Ira Haupt & Co., a bankrupt member), but allowed them only a small fraction of the voting power. A shift is now taking place in the Exchange in response.

These are not matters that an exchange wants to have arbitrated before a congressional committee. Just as the Commission responds to criticism, so does an exchange. The New York Stock Exchange may react to SEC proposals by action and on occasion by forthright opposition. But when the Exchange comes before the Congress and its policies are publicly exposed, its response is likely to be more cooperative. Congressional hearings have a dual effect: they not only keep the Federal agency alert, but they provide some leverage for the agency to prod the exchanges. Thus in turn Congress both directly and indirectly exerts an influence in maintaining the exchanges, the NASD, and the Commission as vital and developing institutions.

RULE MAKING. In the field of rule making by commissions pursuant to statutory authority, Congress is often likely to interfere. Vis-à-vis the FCC, the radio and television industry can, through its networks and local stations, exert enormous political pressure. It controls access of members of Congress to the voters. The stations can support or oppose a candidate; they can offer free time and coverage. Their power would be quite enough without the additional fact that some congressmen actually have a financial interest in them. For these reasons there are few more powerful influences upon Congress. The result is that much of the effort of the FCC resembles the launching of trial balloons, only to find them punctured by a congressional committee. The common technique of a committee or its chairman who opposes a proposed rule is to say that the Commission is exceeding its authority.

BROADCAST COMMERCIALS. One of the best illustrations was in

---

* This includes specialists and the two odd-lot firms.

1963, when the FCC proposed to make rules relating to the length or frequency of broadcast commercials.[36] At that time the Commission pointed out that while broadcasting without advertising would not exist, yet excessive commercials were not in the public interest. It said further, "Our case by case treatment of the problem, however, has not been satisfactory. Recently we have noted a large number of applications for broadcast authorization which presented serious problems of over-commercialization, and coupled with this, our files are replete with substantial complaints from the public. . . ." Therefore, the formal proposal on which public comment was sought was the adoption of a rule requiring all broadcasting stations to observe the limitations on advertising time already contained in the radio and television codes of the National Association of Broadcasters. In this way, the FCC was attempting to make compulsory, as Federal rules, certain provisions already voluntarily agreed upon by many of the broadcasters themselves. This proposal met with widespread opposition from the industry, which quickly reflected itself in strong congressional reaction.

Hearings were therefore held before the House Committee, and its report concluded: [37]

> In the final analysis, it is the judgment of the community which determines whether a broadcaster meets community needs. . . .
>
> Self-regulation by industry is an accepted and valuable supplemental regulatory tool, the effective use of which should be encouraged rather than discouraged.
>
> The adoption by rule of compulsory standards, on the other hand, applicable to all stations or any class of stations as proposed by the Commission would substitute Commission judgment for individual licensee judgment regarding the licensee's day-to-day responsibility of serving the community which he is licensed to serve. . . .

---

[36] Amendment of Part 3 of FCC's Rules and Regulations with respect to advertising on Standard, FM, and Television Broadcast stations, Notice of Proposed Rule-making, FCC, 1963, FCC Release No. 63–467 (May 5, 1963).
[37] House Committee on Interstate and Foreign Commerce, *Lack of Authority of Federal Communications Commission to Make Rules Relating to the Length or Frequency of Broadcast Commercials,* H.R. REP. No. 1054, 88th Cong., 1st Sess. (Dec. 17, 1963), pp. 5–7.

Therefore, in order to protect this regulatory scheme from being transformed by the Commission rules into a totally different regulatory scheme not contemplated by the Congress, it is necessary for the Congress to limit explicitly the scope of the Commission's powers in this respect. . . .

The Commission, after holding oral arguments in the instant rule-making proceeding (docket No. 15083), has voted to abandon the proposed rules limiting the frequency of broadcast commercials. The notion has been advanced by the members of the Commission and by others that under these circumstances the legislation is moot. Nothing can be further from the truth. The instant rulemaking proceeding constitutes an outstanding example of a regulatory agency arrogating to itself the right to legislate. Instead of carrying out the mandate of the Congress, the agency has proposed by Commission fiat to change the regulatory scheme enacted by the Congress.

On January 15, 1964, the Commission unanimously decided to terminate its rule making proceeding.[38] It noted the almost unanimous opposition generated in the broadcasting industry and the rather limited support manifested by members of the public. Notwithstanding the formal termination of the rule making proceeding, H.R. 8316 was brought to a vote in the House on February 27, 1964, and passed by a vote of 317 to 43.[39] Regardless of one's views on the merits respecting broadcast commercials, should we quarrel with the power or propriety of Congress' expressing a negative view? Clearly not. This is direct and explicit legislative revision.

SUBSCRIPTION TELEVISION. Pay television is another area in which Congress took issue with the FCC. In its first report on subscription television the question before the Commission was whether licensees should be authorized to transmit programs whose reception by the public would require a charge.[40] Rather

---

[38] Amendment of Part 3 of the Commission's Rules and Regulations with respect to advertising on Standard, FM, and Television Broadcast Stations, 29 FED. REG. 503, 1 R.R. 2d 1606 (1964).

[39] 110 CONG. REC. 3909 (1964).

[40] In the Matter of Amendment of Part 3 of the Commission's Rules and Regulations (Radio Broadcast Services) to provide for Subscription Television Service, First Report, 23 FCC 532, 16 R.R. 1509 (1957).

than permitting widespread licensing at one extreme or forbidding the service entirely, the Commission took a median position and concluded that "it is not possible . . . without a demonstration of the service in operation to determine reliably where the practical realities lie." As a consequence, the FCC authorized a trial for subscription television in three markets.

The release of the first report in 1957 led to intensified efforts on the part of opponents of subscription television.[41] The charge was made that it would gravely impair free television service provided to the public, and further that the FCC proposals would permit or foster monopolistic control. To marshal opposition, broadcasters and theater owners got in touch directly with congressmen, and organized a massive publicity effort encouraging large numbers of viewers to express their fears and objections. In 1958 the House committee held hearings and adopted resolutions opposing the experiment, stating that it should not proceed unless and until the Communications Act was amended specifically to permit authorization of subscription television. A similar position was taken by the Senate committee. Although Congress adjourned without passing any legislation, Chairman Harris requested that the Commission maintain the *status quo* to permit consideration of pending bills in the next session of Congress. Early in 1959 agreement was reached between the Commission and the House committee on a subscription television experiment much narrower in scope than the one proposed in the first report. There was never legislation, but in a subsequent ("third") report [42] the Commission itself said that it would be "preferable to limit the trial of any particular subscription television system using broadcast facilities to a single market." Chairman Harris described the history of the pay television controversy in the Congressional Record as follows: [43]

It was the testimony of most of the witnesses who appeared before our committee that the scope of the tests contemplated by the

[41] See generally JONES, CASES AND MATERIALS ON REGULATED INDUSTRIES, ch. 10 (to be published by Foundation Press, Inc., in 1967).

[42] Amendment of Part 3 of the Commission's Rules and Regulations (Radio Broadcast Services) to provide for Subscription, Third Report, 16 R.R. 1540*a* (Released by FCC on March 24, 1959).

[43] 105 CONG. REC. 5362–5363 (1959).

Commission in its first report was so broad that there was a grave risk that these tests would bring about the virtual establishment of a new subscription television service on some extended or permanent basis without the Congress having an opportunity to consider whether the operation of such a service on a permanent basis was in the public interest.

The tests proposed by the Commission in its third report are considerably more limited. Such tests would be conducted only in cities which have at least four commercial television services—including the applicant's station. There are 20 cities meeting this specific requirement. . . .

Under these circumstances, the committee . . . adopted a resolution to the effect that the earlier resolution adopted by the committee . . . should not apply to the subscription television test operations contemplated by the Commission's third report. . . .

All that is authorized is the conduct of limited tests sufficient to determine the feasibility of subscription television. . . .

Unlike the case of TV commercials, might this be described as pressure through the committee rather than Congress—acting through legislation? *

DEINTERMIXTURE. A similar congressional reaction was evident when the FCC decided on a selective basis to require six communities to operate with only ultra high frequency (UHF) stations, and to reject the location of any VHF station there.[44] The Commission's ultimate objective was to increase the number of broadcasting stations in the country by expanding the use of UHF bands, since there are relatively few VHF channels available. This FCC requirement (known technically as selective "deintermixture") met with broad opposition from the communities affected, and also from Congress. As a consequence, and because of the pressure from the House committee, a compromise was reached pursuant to which Congress passed the "All Channel Receiver" legislation sought by the Commission (on July 10, 1962).[45] This bill empowered the FCC to require that

---

* The pay television issue is not closed. In April, 1966, it was revived by an FCC proposal that over-the-air subscription television be authorized on a permanent and nationwide basis.

[44] See generally Note, *The Darkened Channels: UHF Television and the FCC*, 75 HARV. L. REV. 1578 (1962).

[45] 76 STAT. 150, 47 U.S.C.A. § 303(s) (1962).

television sets be capable of receiving all frequencies—including both UHF and VHF. In order to obtain favorable legislation on the "All Channel Receiver Bill," the Commission had to agree to suspend its deintermixture efforts, except in four cases far advanced in the decisional process. In dropping the cases already initiated, it concluded that the new legislation "eliminated the need to resort to these other stimuli" to achieve UHF development. This was a compromise in which the Commission obtained a legislative solution which it had long sought.[46]

FPC JURISDICTION. A more dramatic illustration of combined industry and committee pressure has been recorded in relation to the Federal Power Commission in 1947. The issue then before the Supreme Court [47] was whether the Commission possessed the power to regulate wholesale sales of natural gas to pipe-line companies which transport it in interstate commerce for resale to the public (when nothing further in the gathering process remains to be done). The natural gas industry was outraged at this possibility. Acting through Congressman Ross Rizley of Oklahoma it pushed a bill [48] through the House that the Interstate Commerce Committee of the Senate refused to report out. Yet according to some critics the industry's indignation was so effective that it intimidated the FPC and forced it to back away from asserting jurisdiction where the sales were to be made by independent producers. The Supreme Court unanimously sustained the Commission's power despite its reluctance. In the words of Professor A. L. Scanlan: [49]

> On the eve of Supreme Court's action on the *Interstate* case, we are presented with the unusual spectacle of an administrative agency

[46] The background is explained in excerpts from the House Committee report on the bill. H.R. REP. No. 1559, 87th Cong., 2d Sess. (1962), pp. 4–5; see also *id.* at pp. 18–26 (letter from the FCC to Representative Harris) and S. REP. No. 1526, 87th Cong., 2nd Sess. (1962), pp. 13–19 (letter from the FCC to Senator Pastore).

[47] See *Interstate Natural Gas Company, Inc. v. FPC*, 330 U.S. 852 (1947) (*cert. granted but Supreme Court review limited to certain specific issues*).

[48] H.R. 2185, 80th Cong., 1st Sess. (1947).

[49] Scanlan, *Administrative Abnegation in the Face of Congressional Coercion: The Interstate Natural Gas Company Affair*, 23 NOTRE DAME LAW. 173, at 194–195 (1947).

frantically trying to vitiate the charges hurled at them by the natural-gas industry members and their representatives in Congress by giving up part of their jurisdiction over wholesale sales in interstate commerce, a jurisdiction which was bestowed upon them by the clear language of the Act itself, not to mention the further abundant evidence found in the legislative history of the statute. So intent were they to mollify their critics, that they had agreed in advance that if the Supreme Court should sustain their position they would willingly surrender the fruits of that victory!

The quotation of Mr. Scanlan represents one side. On the other side, it is said that the majority on the Federal Power Commission never believed it should assert such broad jurisdiction under the act. No one, however, denies the attempt of the industry, through Congressman Rizley, to exert maximum influence.

SEC RULE 17a-8. A lesser example of the same anxiety on the part of Congress was experienced by the Securities and Exchange Commission in 1964. In hearings before his committee, Chairman Harris of the Interstate and Foreign Commerce Committee raised a question concerning the adoption by the SEC of a proposal to adopt Rule 17a-8 under the Securities Exchange Act.[50] The proposal, which was not acceptable to the New York Stock Exchange, in general provided that exchanges should be required to file reports of changes in their own rules three weeks in advance of adoption, with a shorter period in emergencies. It expressly provided, however, that the failure on the part of an exchange to file such a report should not affect the validity, force, or effect of its rules or actions. The rule was thus a reporting mechanism adopted pursuant to the Commission's broad authority to require reports, and our Commission had concluded that it was well within the express grant of rule making power and also entirely consistent with the statutory scheme of self-regulation under Commission oversight. It would give the SEC some knowledge in advance of what an exchange was proposing to do and thus permit discussion. On the other hand, the Commission recognized that it had no power to approve or disapprove an exchange rule directly. Its only power is to request the exchange to make a

---

[50] *House Hearings* [pt. 2, Investor Protection] (Feb. 5, 1964), p. 1132.

specified change, and after appropriate notice and opportunity for hearing, make a finding that such a change is necessary and appropriate for the protection of investors, which finding may be appealed to the Federal courts.

Although Chairman Harris at the time was critical of the New York Stock Exchange and therefore was not taking sides to defend its practices, nevertheless he reminded our Commission that its own Special Study report [51] had included the statement that "The Exchange Act does not require Exchanges to file rule changes prior to adoption." They may adopt a rule, but the SEC is authorized to require changes after due notice, hearing, and appropriate findings. He therefore construed the proposed Rule 17a-8 as an effort on the part of the Commission to do what it had admitted it does not have authority to do, and said:[52]

> They are going to reach it in a different way, which is a thing that disturbs me about many of these regulatory agencies.
>
> I support their efforts to administer the law as was intended but I do raise questions in which they acknowledge that they do not have the authority in a certain realm and then get about and devise ways and means that they can come around some other way and say they are going to do it in another way, they did not have authority to do it (sic).

Chairman Harris' criticism raised a difficult problem for a regulatory agency, particularly when it was in the bind of attempting to get through his committee a bill of the highest importance. Nevertheless we decided that our authority to require reports was adequately broad and clear, and we therefore went ahead and adopted the rule. I then received a letter dated March 9 from the chairman, as follows:

> Although I have no further comment to make at this time beyond that I made during the course of the hearings on February 6, 1964, I wish you to know that I am not unaware of the fact that on March 3 the Commission adopted Rule 17a-8.

---

[51] *Special Study*, pt. 5, p. 200 (1963).
[52] *House Hearings* [pt. 2, Investor Protection] (Feb. 5, 1964) p. 1132.

This was a calculated risk on the part of our Commission but happily it did not yield bitter fruit.

Taking action in the face of a chairman's objection, however, cannot be construed as a consistent practice on the part of the SEC or any other regulatory commission. It may seem lacking in courage, but I believe it is safe to conclude that agencies seldom take controversial steps under their rule making power which do not have some support from Congress. In view of his almost autocratic powers, the committee chairman's views are likely to be given extraordinary weight.

FTC CIGARETTE RULE. In other areas Congress has demonstrated its control over regulatory agencies by specifically legislating against actions already taken. This is widely done and is certainly the most clear-cut and definite expression of public disagreement —either nullifying a commission rule or taking away its jurisdiction. A recent illustration arose out of the report of the Surgeon General of the Public Health Service on January 11, 1964, which made the finding that "Cigarette smoking is a health hazard of sufficient importance . . . to warrant appropriate remedial action." On the basis of that report the FTC issued a notice of proposed rule making to the effect that labeling and advertising of cigarettes must contain a warning of the health hazard. There is a substantial basis for inferring that such a rule was not encouraged by the White House, but the FTC nevertheless persevered. It is another example of "independence" discussed in Chapter 1. Specifically the rule, as finally adopted on June 22, 1964, provided [53] that "it is an unfair or deceptive act or practice . . . to fail to disclose, clearly and prominently, in all advertising and on every pack or other container . . . that cigarette smoking is dangerous to health and may cause death from cancer and other diseases." The basis and purpose of the rule and the Commission's authority to issue it were carefully developed in an accompanying statement. In the words of Professor Kenneth C. Davis,[54] "Even if Congress overrides it, as seems likely, I think the FTC opinion is a masterful contribution to administrative law and that it may be

[53] 29 FED. REG. 8325 (1964).
[54] DAVIS, TEACHER'S MANUAL TO ADMINISTRATIVE LAW CASEBOOK, p. 5 (1965 ed.).

one of the outstanding administrative opinions of the 20th century."

As might have been anticipated, opposition did arise particularly out of the tobacco states, and the House Interstate and Foreign Commerce Committee directed its chairman to request that the FTC postpone the effective date of the rule from January to July of 1965, which the FTC accepted. In the following session Congress enacted Public Law 89-92,[55] which would supersede the commission's rule because, as stated in the House report: "The Committee feels that at the present time the necessity for, and the effectiveness of this requirement has not been demonstrated." Relying on the fact that the cigarette industry had appointed a czar over its advertising, the new law requires that packages should contain the following statement: "Caution: Cigarette smoking may be hazardous to your health."

Comments on the bill on the House floor were sharp on both sides.[56] Representative Udall (Democrat, Arizona) said it "should be entitled 'A Bill for the relief and protection of the tobacco industry,'" and Congressman Moss (Democrat, California) pointed out that it was merely a warning "in whispered tones" to the smoker "who is already hooked," to which Congressman Cooley (Democrat, North Carolina) replied, "What kind of a label do you want to put on there? A skull and bones?" A *New York Times* editorial at the time (July 9, 1965) was highly critical: [57]

> Congress has now virtually completed action on a shocking piece of special interest legislation in this field. . . .
>
> The central issue now confronting the President is the integrity and independence of the Federal Trade Commission. What possible objective justification can there be for Congress intervening to strip a regulatory agency of its authority over a particular industry? This bill confers a favor on one industry that all the other industries under the commission's jurisdiction would naturally like to have.
>
> Sound governmental practice requires a veto of this bill. Other-

---

[55] 89th Cong., 1st Sess. (July 14, 1965).

[56] 111 Cong. Rec. 15959–15963 (daily ed. July 13, 1965).

[57] Editorial, "Cigarettes v. F.T.C.," N.Y. Times, July 9, 1965.

wise, the President and Congress will be flashing a green signal to the lobbyists that any regulatory agency is open to invasion and emasculation.

Does this editorial say too much? Should we not separate procedure from the merits? In all probability the tobacco lobby should not have prevailed. But upon a "limelight" issue receiving national attention, can we say that Congress has usurped jurisdiction from an agency by legislation that prescribes another standard?

HEARINGS ON MATTERS IN ADJUDICATION. *Ex parte* influence affecting the adjudicatory process will be noted in Chapter 5. It was the subject of congressional inquiry in the Eisenhower administration and has resulted in the establishment of formal codes of behavior. We were the beneficiaries of the public criticism and concern during the late fifties.

However, a related form of congressional pressure has been noted in the press and in a 1966 court decision. It has been applied openly by a committee (as distinguished from an individual congressman) to a matter then being adjudicated. It is not entirely novel: a study was made in 1960 of congressional committee influence on Labor Board proceedings.[58]

According to the *New York Times* of January 15, 1966,[59] Congressman Wright Patman, chairman of the House Banking and Currency Committee and one of the most sulfurous members of the House, was opposed to the banks offering interests in a pooled investment (in effect, a mutual fund), a subject already referred to earlier in this chapter in the section on The Budget, page 39. He asked the SEC, which is not under the jurisdiction of his committee, to delay its decision on the application of the First National City Bank of New York for certain exemptions in creating and managing a mutual fund (more explicitly, in registering the interests to be sold under the Securities Act and the Investment Company Act). The approaches of the Commission and Mr. Patman are entirely different: the SEC insisted that an inter-

---

[58] Scher, *Congressional Committee Members as Independent Agency Overseers: A Case Study*, 54 AM. POL. SCI. REV. 911 (1960).

[59] N.Y. Times, Jan. 15, 1966, p. 31, col. 7.

est in a pooled investment is a security which falls within its juris-diction and must be registered, but unlike Chairman Patman, took no position on its propriety or legality under the Banking Act of 1933 once it was registered. Perhaps, therefore, a congressional hearing in this case could be reconciled with the continuation of a formal SEC proceeding. The difficulty, however, would arise if the SEC were called to testify before Congressman Patman's committee in connection with the proposal of the First National City Bank that was presently before it. The Commission's position would inevitably be the subject for discussion.[60]

This problem had already been aired (on January 7, 1966) by the United States Court of Appeals for the Fifth Circuit in the case of *The Pillsbury Company v. Federal Trade Commission.*[61] The complaint there sought divestiture by Pillsbury of two other companies it had acquired, and the FTC had so ordered. While the case was pending, the Chairman of the Federal Trade Commission was required to testify before the Senate Subcommittee on Antitrust and Monopoly and to state his opinions concerning the enforcement of the Celler-Kefauver Anti-merger Act of 1950 and Section 7 of the Clayton Act. Chairman Howrey's views were solicited specifically with respect to the Pillsbury situation. The court decided that the order of the Federal Trade Commission must be vacated, and said: [62]

> We conclude that the proceedings just outlined constituted an improper intrusion into the adjudicatory processes of the commission and were of such a damaging character as to have required at least some of the members in addition to the chairman to disqualify themselves.

The thrust of this decision is that congressional interference by way of hearings in a matter then before a regulatory agency is improper and may have the consequence of invalidating the action taken.

---

[60] The matter was decided by the SEC. In the Matter of First National City Bank, Investment Company Act Release No. 4538 (Mar. 9, 1966).
[61] 354 F. 2d 952 (5th Cir. 1966).
[62] *Id.* at 963.

## Conclusion

In reassessing the examples and attempting to generalize from them, congressional participation appears to fall into several different categories. Whatever our views may be on the merits, certainly legislative reversal (as in the case of broadcast commercials and the cigarette rule) seems proper. Pressures of this type, of course, are an essential feature of the democratic process. What Congress has given, it may take away. Furthermore, when Congress has been aroused, rightly or wrongly, to the point where it formally legislates against action taken by a regulatory agency, then it is time for a commission to desist. An agency should still feel free to persevere in an attempt to persuade Congress that it was wrong. Yet it seems clear that any responsible commission must cease any effort to harass industry to obtain the same result by oblique means despite a legislative mandate to the contrary. (I make this point, and emphasize it, because some dedicated civil servants sometimes never give up in what they conceive to be the public interest.)

On the other hand, unilateral committee or committee chairman action (as in the case of FPC jurisdiction, subscription TV, and some Appropriations Committee reports) seems doubtful and in fact improper. At this level, industry pressure can be overwhelming. This is notably true, as already shown, in the case of the FCC and FPC. To put it another way, a committee chairman or even a powerful member of a committee who has one constituent back home can create far more havoc with a commission proposal or decision than his constituent's role in the economy would justify. One of my colleagues has suggested a distinction between matters in the limelight (such as regulation of natural gas and cigarette advertising), where there is a public controversy, and those of a more technical nature. The latter being less in the public eye, congressional "policy" may be a product solely of industry pressure applied to a committee or a powerful member such as the chairman.

The pressure applied through holding a congressional hearing when a matter is formally before a commission is also to be condemned. On the border line are cases where the commission

57

yielded on one substantive policy to secure favorable action on another.

In the light of the foregoing limited examples, the conclusion might be drawn that Congress has relatively little interest in encouraging a regulatory agency to perform its function dynamically, but is vitally concerned over any action to which its constituents object. At the same time, it would be unfair to characterize this attitude as purely "negative," for the negative aspect is a mode of protection of an industry and the companies within it by forcing a reexamination of rulemaking and adjudication. This definitely has a conservatizing influence upon the commission but is not always harmful. Perhaps the SEC was fortunate, but the impact of Congress from 1961 to 1964 was helpful. Despite frustrations and unfair treatment at its hands, the regulatory agencies can in some cases benefit from the role of Congress in its oversight capacity.

If we look at these examples from the viewpoint of a commission, it seems clear that regulatory agencies do not have so much power as they are thought to have. Collectively, as a group of commissions, they do cover a wide spectrum of cases involving many industries and companies within them. In other words, the total impact is substantial when all the orders and the cases are bundled together. However, as far as any policy making by an agency is concerned, it seems clear that any major move is subjected to minute scrutiny by Congress. As one congressman said to me in connection with our hearings, "First of all, I always look to see if there are any letters in my file concerning the agency before us."

Finally, much comment has been made over the fact that these agencies are "independent" and therefore there is no accountability. The facts of the matter are that a very substantial measure of accountability is present through the oversight power of Congress and the existence of committee staffs who in many cases have demonstrated competence. The regulatory agencies are more frequently before Congress than any unit of a large executive department which may be making comparable decisions affecting a firm or an entire region. This oversight power is essential to maintain the proper balance of power in the agencies. When Congress finally passed the Securities Acts Amendments of 1964, it inserted a provision to the effect that "The Commission shall include in its annual reports to the Congress for the fiscal years ended on June 30 of 1965, 1966, and 1967 information, data, and recommendations specifically related to the operation of the amendments to this Act. . . ." [63] The committee report adds: [64]

> The committee intends to continue its watchfulness of just what is accomplished to achieve this protection, and for this reason has included in the bill the specific requirement that the Commission report in each of the next 3 years just how effective the amendments proposed by this bill have been to achieve the goal sought.

This was a caveat. Yet it can be a healthy opportunity to air the problems of the agency vis-à-vis the industry, as well as industry complaints about the agencies.

---

[63] Section 20(c) of the Securities Exchange Act of 1934, as amended.
[64] H.R. Rep. No. 1418, 88th Cong., 2d Sess. (May 19, 1964), p. 8.

## 3 | *The Vitality of a*

## *Regulatory Agency*

IF we review the major forces at work upon a regulatory agency the analogy to a stepchild of both Congress and the Executive seems appropriate: its custody is contested on the floor of Congress, and yet there is no deep concern over its needs or its future. Under these circumstances, the initial question still remains relevant: How can an agency avoid a pedestrian, though fair and honest, administration of its functions?

In handling a large part of the agency's business (viz., registration statements, proxy material, routine orders and advisory opinions), competence and faithfulness, coupled with experience, are about all that can be expected. The margin of success lies in the way the other part is administered. To meet this challenge imagination and leadership are not always enough. Sometimes the answer is that little more is possible, because of a straitened budget and the temper of the times.

### *Obstacles to Vitality*

On occasion, however, the opportunity may arise, but when it does, several ingredients are called into play. One element that is most needed is a political and economic climate that will evoke special interest in the agency's role, on the part of the public and of Congress. For example, the stock market may be dropping or gyrating because of alleged activity by speculators, and Congress will look to the SEC. The public may be dissatisfied with the television available to it, and attention will focus on the FCC. A forecast may be published of a shortage in electric power, or a blackout may happen on the Eastern seaboard, and the President will turn to the FPC. Or, again, air transport service may not meet the demand and the CAB will be called upon to resolve it.

Parallel with a special interest in the commission is the need for a program which can appeal to both Congress and the public, can excite young recruits, and finally can be made palatable to the industry subject to regulation.

The third element is the availability of funds, in large part a function of the other two. Additional money for regulatory agencies, traditionally starved since the beginning of the war, cannot be anticipated unless the problems and programs of the agency are in some way dramatized.

In connection with the Securities and Exchange Commission, several factors worked in our favor in the spring of 1961. Probably most important was that there were fewer obstacles to overcome than exist in sister agencies. One of them, standing in the way of some agencies, is the concept accepted in Congress and the White House that there should be a balanced commission. I know this point of view exists at times in the White House, and the phrase has been most recently used by President Johnson in discussing a 1964 appointment to the SEC (see below). As noted in Chapter 2, it is clearly in the mind of Congress, which frequently regards the agencies solely as judicial bodies charged with rendering evenhanded justice. The problem is most acute in the case of agencies such as the Federal Power Commission and the Federal Communications Commission, where political pressures can be most readily identified and exerted. It is very difficult, for example, to administer a program involving the fixing of gas rates in the Southwest when the Power Commission is equally divided between persons speaking for oil and gas interests and those representing the consuming public, primarily in the large urban and industrial centers.

In 1965 this issue was highlighted in news headlines over the filling of vacancies in the FPC. There was widespread speculation whether President Johnson would reappoint Charles R. Ross, who was regarded as consumer-minded and thus opposed by gas interests. His term expired June 22, 1964, but he stayed on, the law permitting a commissioner to remain until his successor takes office.

The President delayed for months. Then, when an unexpected vacancy occurred on the FPC in August, with the death of Commissioner Harold C. Woodward, Mr. Ross' chances of reappointment improved. According to the *Wall Street Journal*,[1] "the reasoning in industry circles was that the President could satisfy consumer groups by naming Mr. Ross and at the same time naming an industry-oriented commissioner to replace Mr. Woodward." Simultaneously, on March 21, 1965, the President announced the selection of Mr. Ross and of Carl E. Bagge, sponsored by Senator Dirksen (the Republican minority leader) and an attorney for a Western railway who described himself as a "pragmatic conservative."

Thus the issue was left hanging and the reappointment of Chairman Swidler became the pivotal point. Mr. Swidler, a long-term public servant and former counsel to TVA, was regarded upon his original selection by President Kennedy as "pro-consumer." His term expired in June, 1965. Again the choice of a successor dangled, for Mr. Swidler, an independent and remarkably effective chairman, had previously indicated to the President that he did not wish to seek reappointment. When he was about to retire, the President urged him to remain for awhile to provide further time to find a successor. Shortly afterwards, the power failure and blackout in the Northeast occurred and there was a dire need for someone of Mr. Swidler's unique experience in TVA to investigate its causes and make recommendations. Mr. Swidler did stay until January, 1966, when his study of the power issue had been completed. According to the *New York Times* of January 23, 1966: [2]

---

[1] "Johnson Fills Posts at NLRB, CAB and FPC," Wall Street Journal, March 22, 1965, p. 2, col. 2.

[2] "Potomac Puzzle: Next FPC Chief," N.Y. Times, Jan. 23, 1966, § 3, p. 4, col. 1.

Mr. Swidler . . . finally achieved the impossible: He left with the praises of both consumer groups and industry ringing in his ears. . . .

Whomever President Johnson names, the appointment is likely to be criticized, for at least one of the sides in the controversies with which the commission deals will like the new man less than they liked Mr. Swidler—and both sides conceivably could be disappointed.

It is not unlikely that the criticism of the White House implicit in the *New York Times* article might have had an effect on the President. Finally in February, 1966, the President announced the appointment of Lee C. White, special counsel in the White House.[3] In characterizing him, labels such as "liberal" are rather loosely used in the press. Nevertheless, as a one-time member of Mr. Swidler's staff at the TVA, Mr. White was put in the ranks of those favoring consumers. Thus the scales remained tipped in their direction.

In an analogous situation the *New York Times* questioned the appointment of an SEC commissioner in 1964 on the claim that he was an archconservative and labeled it, erroneously, as a portent of a changing attitude (against vigorous regulation).[4] President Johnson reacted strongly, and expressed the view that a "balanced" commission would be achieved. He then filled other vacancies with an honored and long-term SEC career public servant as chairman and an able securities lawyer from California.[5]

With this attitude toward maintaining balance, it might be well to ask how a program can ever be adopted which faces squarely the basic underlying problems of the industry. I do not believe a President can afford to ignore balance entirely. Much of the work of a commission is quasi-judicial, and calls for opinion from all sides. Different points of view are helpful also in policy making,

---

[3] "Lee C. White, Nominated to Head FPC, Likely to Avoid Drastic Reshaping of Laws," Wall Street Journal, Feb. 14, 1966, p. 3, col. 2; N.Y. Times, Feb. 12, 1966, p. 1, col. 1.

[4] Editorial, "An Unprofessional Appointment," N.Y. Times, June 9, 1964.

[5] N.Y. Times, July 11, 1964, p. 1, col. 2.

through rules or otherwise. Yet what with vacancies and sickness in the membership, a perfectly balanced, i.e., evenly divided, commission can often be achieved, but at a cost: it tends to make any vigorous administration impossible.

In the case of a commission such as the FCC having seven members, which is much too large to be manageable, balance has also been a problem. According to some critics, there has been constant difficulty in mobilizing a majority who would favor the exercise of any substantial controls over broadcasters. Even when a policy position is finally adopted by a majority and is to be executed through rule making rather than the adjudicatory process, the problem of justifying such a rule before Congress, with one's colleagues openly in opposition, creates embarrassment. It has been an unhappy tradition in Congress and even at broadcasters' conventions for the FCC commissioners to appear and be polled, or at least asked to express their individual views, extemporaneously. This practice was deplored by Chairman Oren Harris.[6]

In the case of the SEC, although some colleagues are more conservative than others, there is not usually so clear a line between persons who are "pro industry" or "pro regulation." "Balance" in the SEC thus is not so meaningful as in some other agencies. The line between "liberals" and "conservatives" is an oversimplification because many "conservative" people may regard securities violations as so serious and so reprehensible as to warrant immediate intervention on the part of government.

In considering "balance" and potential differences within the commission, I minimize the role of political affiliation. During the Kennedy years neither Newton Minow, Chairman of the FCC, nor Alan Boyd, Chairman of the CAB, would have mustered adequate support without some of their Republican colleagues. Indeed, many of their Democratic members were in the opposition. An incoming chairman can achieve far more by appreciating the talents and experience available, including his predecessor in office (who may remain as commissioner), than by adopting an immediate "new broom" approach. If one's predecessors are hon-

---

[6] See Harris' Speech before the United States Chamber of Commerce, Fourth Annual Public Affairs Conference, Washington, D.C., Feb. 4, 1965.

orable and able men, as were the four who had been chairmen of the SEC during the Eisenhower administration,[7] it is either pious or naïve, or both, to do otherwise.

Perhaps the greatest tribulations during the 1962 to 1964 period were borne by Mr. Swidler in dealing with a commissioner of his own party. As noted earlier in this chapter, Mr. Swidler was regarded with some suspicion in the gas industry as "consumer oriented." Yet in January, 1963, his colleague Commissioner Howard V. Morgan, one-time Oregon Utility Commissioner, made public a copy of a letter sent to President Kennedy asking not to be considered for reappointment when his term expired and implying that the FPC was dominated by the public utility interests.[8] A strong advocate of public power, Mr. Morgan claimed that the FPC had declined to investigate some cases because "it would disturb the industry," [9] and said that "ordinary men yield too quickly to the present-day urge toward conformity, timidity and personal security." [10] In a hearing before the House Interstate and Foreign Commerce Committee, he complained of FPC procedures and said they had cost the consumers millions of dollars a year in gas and electric rate charges, and attributed them to "lack of freedom of action and independence, the appointment of the commission chairman by the President, and the chairman's complete administrative control." Finally, he claimed that the heavy burden of cases leaves "the way open for the commissioners to become captives of the staff, who are captives of the chairman, who in turn is a captive of the White House." [11] Chairman Swidler was forced to defend the FPC record at a news conference, where he attributed Mr. Morgan's dissidence to personality differences.[12] In a subsequent hearing, under questioning, he testified that Mr. Morgan might have been politically motivated in his dissents and in writing to the President. He said he thought

---

[7] The four immediate predecessors were Edward N. Gadsby, Ralph H. Demmler, J. Sinclair Armstrong, and Donald C. Cook.

[8] N.Y. Times (Western Ed.), Jan. 26, 1963; p. 1, col. 4.

[9] N.Y. Times (Western Ed.), Feb. 28, 1963; p. 1, col. 2.

[10] N.Y. Times (Western Ed.), *Ibid.*

[11] N.Y. Times (Western Ed.), March 1, 1963; p. 11, col. 6 and p. 14, col. 1.

[12] N.Y. Times (Western Ed.), Jan. 31, 1963; p. 9, col. 2.

Mr. Morgan had in mind "campaigning for the governorship." [13]

Here is a brilliant demonstration of the fact that differences between members of the same party can be far greater than between representatives of different parties. Suffice it to say, Mr. Morgan was not urged to remain.

In the case of the SEC it is probably accidental that my Republican colleagues were more conservative and certainly more resolute in their views than the rest. Yet being persons of immense integrity, ability, and experience, they appreciated the essential problems of the securities industry. Despite heated debate within the commission and with those undertaking the Special Study of the Securities Markets, we never suffered any loss of mutual respect, and hammered out our conclusions. Thus, happily, when we went before Congress I was able to have a united front, a helpful and in some cases essential ingredient to getting legislative support.

A second obstacle to overcome is the tendency toward overjudicialization. It exists in most commissions to some extent. It is clear that the SEC had not used all its legislative (rule making) powers pursuant to the authority of a general statute. We were in danger of thinking too much in judicial terms. Yet much of our commission were, or through the Special Study became, consciously aware of the danger in overjudicialization. A former chairman of another agency has described it thus: "I think that several of my fellow members see themselves every day as wandering down the hall with black robes and look at everything they do as if they were judges. Instead of trying to develop basic programs for the industry they are regulating, they feel they have to make every decision on an ad hoc, case-by-case basis. It is hard to elevate them to look at national policy."

Probably judicialization has reached its highest point of fruition in the ICC, already discussed in Chapter 2; The Impasse in the ICC, pages 31 to 35.

Bearing this in mind, during 1961 to 1964 we did our best to keep examining policy as distinguished from limiting ourselves to the decision of cases. Of course, sometimes we recognized that cases themselves might be the best way of articulating new pol-

---

[13] N.Y. Times (Western Ed.), March 2, 1963; p. 1, col. 1.

icy. However, much of our program was one of rule making—exercising existing powers—and we met as long as six hours a day five days a week in order to get to the main issues that the SEC then faced.

A third obstacle that agencies sometimes have to overcome is the claim that they have become captives of the industry. I was personally unaware of this in the SEC or any of the other agencies with which I had any association. Some commissioners, however, should be recognized as "captive" when appointed. Indeed, that is why they were chosen: because of their experience with the industry they were regulating, or perhaps to produce the kind of "balanced commission" already described. By the same token, I know of cases of commissioners (outside the SEC) who were so doctrinaire in their attitude favoring the consumer that they could not take a position favoring the industry which they admitted to be basically sound. They were captives of an ideology. They would say they could not "afford to vote as they chose."

It is interesting to inquire what it really means when we say that an agency or a commissioner has become a "captive" of the industry. Part of it may be hardening of the arteries—lack of initiative in fostering new programs. Part may stem from the fact that the parties are dealing with the industry day to day and begin to appreciate their problems without taking due account of the public interest. Another way of phrasing the same point appeared in the Landis Report: "Irrespective of the absence of social contacts and the absence of undue hospitality, it is the daily machine-gun-like impact on both agency and its staff of industry representation that makes for industry orientation on the part of many honest and capable agency members as well as agency staffs." [14] Still another student of regulatory agencies has said: "By the time you become a real expert, you ought to quit." And finally, part of it may be an actual lack of personal independence on the part of the commissioners, to which I adverted earlier (Chapter 1; Formal Controls by the White House, page 11). Possibility of captive commissioners, in the pejorative sense, seems more likely in the case of state commissioners. I have been informed by several top officials of insurance companies that a few insurance superin-

---

[14] *Landis Report*, p. 71.

tendents in various states are nothing more than spokesmen for the industry (see Chapter 4). I was happy to find this was not evident among the securities commissioners of the states, although it is a sorry sight to find that the annual three-day meeting of the North American Securities Administrators is financed by representatives of the securities industry who come to the meetings in waves. In fact, the hosts far outnumber the administrators they are feting. This is a development which somehow has been permitted to grow, but clearly it should be curbed. In many jurisdictions, securities commissions are hopelessly underpaid, undermanned, and starved for funds. Yet they should not subject themselves to potential criticism, such as is leveled at some state insurance commissions.

Finally, as compared with other regulatory agencies, the SEC has had a tradition and a reputation for service and responsibility, and some reserve of high quality staff members. Back in the 1930s it was one of the two best law offices in Washington, together with the Solicitor General of the United States. I might say this reputation has been partially maintained despite some hardship. Like other institutions, it had its ups and downs with meager budgets following the war; its ranks of competent lawyers and analysts were thinned in the process. While the Commission sought to hold to its standard of competency, it scarcely had time to see that the direction of the industry which it regulated had been changing. Without additional personnel and without fiscal support, the only choice was to meet the grist of day-to-day relations on an *ad hoc* basis.

Thus by way of introduction it can be said that the SEC faced fewer problems in attempting to develop a new program than many other commissions. At the same time, for the SEC as for most institutions, an occasional reexamination was needed. Their job should be to raise standards, not to hold fast to the *status quo*. As already stated earlier in the Introduction, the real fear haunting all administrative agencies should be fear of inertia, the loss of initiative. How can this be surmounted?

### Possible Approaches

In rethinking the problems of the SEC, one example was already available in 1961 to 1962. A novel approach was then being taken in the Federal Communications Commission. The television industry was awakened. Several major FCC bills were passed, and any legislative success in Congress was arduous during the Kennedy administration. Why not, therefore, like Newton Minow, start off by comparing conditions in the securities industry with the vast wasteland of TV programs? [15] The answer was severalfold. First of all, Mr. Minow was operating with commissioners originally unsympathetic with change or at least with the changes he proposed. He had to speak out dramatically, courageously, and alone, or not at all. He could speak, not act. Second, the FCC has relatively limited powers in the vital area of programming; the SEC, on the other hand, has rather broad and general powers, which it had not adequately exercised. Third, a broadside against the TV industry would not have the same effect, psychological or otherwise, as one addressed to an industry so closely tied with the stock market. Such an attack upon the latter was not warranted; but even if it had been, it might have been disastrous in its market impact, and therefore irresponsible.

Finally, as I have already indicated and shall develop further in Chapter 4, I have become convinced that no major step forward can be achieved by an old-line regulatory agency in the absence of support from some of the leaders in the industry it regulates. Certainly our legislation would have been impossible without it. Even as to rule making, if none of the industry's spokesmen feel there is a need and complaints mount, congressmen are likely to intervene and commence inquiry, and a committee may either stall the proposal or kill it, as in the case of the FTC cigarette rule (see Chapter 2; pages 53 to 55). I do not say that a consensus is required, for this ignores the element of leadership. A commission can probe, and sense the existence of support even of persons who do not speak openly; and this may suffice.*

Under these circumstances, it was necessary to take a totally

---

* In the foregoing paragraph I differentiate an old-line agency from a new one having a mission—formed for the very purpose of carrying out a program contrary to the wishes of business. Somewhere in between is the administration of such a law as the Public Utility Holding Company Act of 1935. Highly resented in the utility world, it was nonetheless enforced vigorously and effectively by the SEC.

[15] N.Y. Times, May 10, 1961, p. 1, col. 2.

different tack toward raising standards and shifting direction in the securities industry. Lawyers prefer if possible to take positions on the basis of thorough, fair, and responsible study. It is slower, but any major and abiding shift in thinking within the government is a laborious process at best.

*Consultants.* The first step in the case of the SEC was to bring in some consultants who were both knowledgeable and could afford to take some time off to make recommendations. They were two lawyers (one a professor) and a businessman. The businessman was to insure that there was no waste of manpower observable, and the lawyers were there to inquire where we were going in the administration of the laws under our supervision. One of them, Joseph L. Weiner, had had immense experience with regulatory agencies and generously agreed to be our counsel.

One question was whether any SEC functions should be scrapped. This is a novel inquiry among government institutions, flying in the very face of Parkinson's law.[16] In this connection an analysis was made of an area of regulation which had once—from 1938 to 1945—been our largest and most successful achievement: the Public Utility Holding Company Act. Now that it had fulfilled its basic purposes, the rationalization of an industry, should it be dropped as *functus officio?* I would hesitate to go so far, particularly in the light of the trend of acquisitions among electric utilities since 1965. Or if the Public Utility Holding Company Act should not be jettisoned entirely, should its administration be shifted to the Federal Power Commission, which is charged generally with the regulation of the gas and electric industries? This, we found, was not a matter of logic alone. It was a political question. Many people who before have inveighed against the SEC in its administration of the act prefer a known to an unknown agency, the FPC. The latter could undoubtedly strengthen its hold over the gas and electric utilities if SEC financing powers were coupled with its existing jurisdiction over routes and rates. Opposition to any change began to develop. The question, therefore, was left whether we ought to tamper with the utility act. Is it worthwhile to devote one's energies to ridding an

---

[16] PARKINSON, PARKINSON'S LAW (Houghton Mifflin, 1957).

70

agency of its vestigial duties? It is almost as hard to wipe a statute off the books as it is to enact one, and much less rewarding. More important constructive legislation was needed, and Congress has only limited time for agencies such as the SEC. Therefore, since the Public Utility Holding Company Act inhibits the rebirth of certain abuses, it seemed of value to retain on the books under our aegis, but with a limited amount of regulatory activity. By its very existence, it is a policeman even without aggressive enforcement.

*The Special Study.* The overwhelmingly predominant phase of our reexamination was the Special Study of the Securities Markets authorized by Congress in 1961 and completed on August 8, 1963.[17] To appreciate the motivation of the congressional resolution authorizing the Study, the condition of the securities markets during 1961 must be understood. This was a turbulent market in which a record number of companies, many of them highly speculative, were going to the public for financing. The "hot issue" was prevalent; initial trading markets for many new issues reflected an extravagant premium over the offering price. Price-earnings ratios were at extraordinary levels. Trading volume was soaring, accompanied by noticeably high "fails" to receive or deliver stock certificates. The Commission's enforcement machinery was over-loaded. Criminal references to the Department of Justice and administrative proceedings against brokers were at all-time highs. The most dramatic breakdown in controls was reflected in the SEC investigation of the American Stock Exchange,[18] prompted by the Commission's expulsion of the leading specialist firm of Re, Re & Sagarese.[19] Happily, my predecessor had believed in a vigorous enforcement policy and had instituted action against this firm.

The American Stock Exchange investigation affords an example of alternative regulatory approaches that a commission may take,

[17] See Cary, *The Special Study of Securities Markets of the Securities and Exchange Commission*, 62 MICH. L. REV. 557, 558 (1964).
[18] SEC, STAFF REPORT ON ORGANIZATION, MANAGEMENT AND REGULATION OF CONDUCT OF MEMBERS OF THE AMERICAN STOCK EXCHANGE (1962).
[19] SEC Securities Exchange Act Release No. 6551, May 4, 1961; SEC Securities Exchange Act Release No. 6900, Sept. 21, 1962.

and amplifies a position already taken in this chapter. In a report of January 6, 1962, the SEC staff had conclusively demonstrated the deterioration in standards and responsibility on the part of the American Stock Exchange. The staff report concluded: [20]

> There can be little doubt that in the case of the American Stock Exchange the statutory scheme of self-regulation in the public interest has not worked out in the manner originally envisioned by Congress. The manifold and prolonged abuses by specialists and floor traders and other instances of misconduct described in this report make it clear that the problem goes beyond isolated violations and amounts to a general deficiency of standards and a fundamental failure of controls.

No one has ever attempted to controvert this report. Yet the American Stock Exchange officials appeared before the commission and evidenced their total incapacity to appreciate the gravity of the abuses or their obligation in managing a quasi-public institution.

Under these circumstances, if anyone in government wanted headlines, this was a unique opportunity. Like Galahad, we could have publicly denounced the American Stock Exchange. If the SEC had worried about its "image," we should have brought immediate proceedings and publicly forced through a reorganization plan. Then we might have been hailed as "vigorous and tough"—politically attractive labels. On the other hand, such a step would have had adverse effects. First of all, it would have stifled the initiative for self-regulation, and (as pointed out in Chapter 2; Oversight and Self-regulation, page 43) self-regulation is a unique feature of the securities industry.

The New York Stock Exchange had taken many steps forward in setting standards for the industry. Yet the same firms which were members of both had failed to take any interest in the Amex. As one broker said to me in private: "Why spend any time at the New York Athletic Club if we can play at the Racquet?" However, once this situation was fully appreciated by the ex-

---

[20] Quoted in *Special Study*, pt. 4, p. 579 (1963).

change community, responsible members assumed leadership and reorganized the exchange under the direction of the so-called Levy committee. The American Stock Exchange reframed its constitution, abolished its system of self-perpetuating committees controlled by a small group of specialists, strengthened staff responsibility, and elected an able president.[21] As the Special Study report said,[22] "The accomplishment of this reform appears to be an excellent demonstration of the effectiveness of self-regulation under responsible Exchange leadership and active Commission oversight."

A related reason for permitting the exchange to clean its own house is that by public denunciation the SEC would have established a totally different attitude within the industry. As already indicated, if anything was to be done, particularly if legislation was needed, we needed support from some of the leaders in the industry. It is an oversimplification to lump all the members of the financial community into one group: it is not a phalanx. Some of the responsible representatives appreciate their responsibilities and are likely to work even with a government agency if some line of communication is maintained.

In this context—a record registration of new issues and a turbulent market—the Commission, the self-regulatory agencies, and the industry were overwhelmed with daily administrative problems and were forced to meet issues on an *ad hoc* basis. Thus, it seemed a highly propitious time for a thorough survey of the state of the securities markets and the adequacy of investor protection. Without money and personnel, such an ambitious program would not be possible.

Here in retrospect we were beneficiaries of the wisdom of Congress and an element of luck. The question might have been posed whether the study should be made by Congress or by the SEC. Congressional investigations of regulatory agencies (already discussed in Chapter 2; Substantive Aspects, pages 41 to 43) are, on balance, undoubtedly salutary. Indeed, they may

---

[21] See *id.* at pp. 579–584.
[22] *Id.* at 584.

well be the factor most responsible for keeping agencies from falling asleep, or suffering the fate envisioned by Galbraith. It may also be highly appropriate for Congress to investigate matters which raise novel or broad policy issues or where no other agency with the requisite expertise is available. The Senate hearings which laid the foundations for the Securities Act of 1933 and the Securities Exchange Act of 1934 were undoubtedly of this type. But the question always arises whether a study could be done differently or better. A congressional investigation might have had the tendency of focusing on the SEC rather than upon major developments in the market. Not infrequently general policy inquiries are clouded and confused by examination into particular cases, often stemming from private complaints. The Commission might then have spent most of its time attempting to defend what it had or had not done within the limitations of a straitened budget. Thus the real objective might well have been missed, for we, like the securities industry itself, had been so engrossed that there was neither time nor personnel nor opportunity to back away and ask where the industry was moving and whether present regulations met the changes wrought over thirty years. I look back with thanksgiving, for within a few months after taking office I (as the representative of the SEC) might have been the subject (and the target) of congressional inquiry rather than the securities industry. This is the irony of public office.

On August 24, 1961, Congressman Peter Mack introduced a resolution [23] (now section 19(d) of the Securities Exchange Act) authorizing and directing the Commission "to make a study and investigation of the adequacy for the protection of the investors, of the rules of the . . . exchanges and the national securities associations. . . ." The Mack resolution provided a vehicle for re-examination by the commission. Naturally, therefore, we seized upon it as the opportunity for which we were seeking. We said before the House Subcommittee: [24]

---

[23] H.R.J. Res. 438, 87th Cong., 1st Sess. (1961), which became law, 75 Stat. 465 (1961), as 19(d) of the Securities Exchange Act, as amended.
[24] *Hearings on H.R.J. Res. 438 Before a Subcommittee of the House Committee on Interstate and Foreign Commerce,* 87th Cong., 1st Sess. (June 27, 1961), p. 8.

Our present budget . . . and our manpower, will not support a thorough study of the exchanges and over-the-counter markets at this time. . . . [T]he constant danger in our Commission is that with market activities and flotations at an all time high, we become so overwhelmed with immediate problems . . . that we are virtually forced to concentrate all our funds and manpower upon them and cannot do any long-range planning.

As already noted, the Study of some 3,000 pages under the superlative direction of Milton H. Cohen, a Chicago lawyer, was submitted to Congress in the late summer of 1963. Its breadth may perhaps be appreciated by a notation of the range of its subject matter: [25] qualification standards for those in the securities industry; selling and investment advisory practices; distributions of securities, including problems of "hot issues"; intrastate and real estate offerings; the operation of the various securities markets, such as the New York Stock Exchange, the regional exchanges, the "third market" (i.e., the trading of listed securities off the exchanges), and the over-the-counter market, and the interrelationship of these markets; the obligations of issuers of both listed and unlisted publicly held securities; the gaps and inconsistencies in securities credit regulation; selected aspects of mutual funds; and the operation of self-regulation.

Following the Study, substantial progress was made. It gave rise to a bill which became law on August 20, 1964.[26] The history of the Securities Acts Amendments of 1964 will be discussed in Chapter 4. It is not the purpose of this chapter to enumerate all the beneficial results of the Special Study. Suffice it to say, during the fiscal year June 1963–1964, steps were taken to develop: a basis for improved selling practices; a minimum net capital requirement for broker-dealers; qualification standards and rules of conduct for those broker-dealers who were not members of a registered securities association; new rules and responsibilities for specialists on the exchanges and also for floor traders operating for their own account (shrinking the latter from 300 to 30); and

---

[25] See generally Cary, *Administrative Agencies and the Securities and Exchange Commission*, 29 LAW & CONTEMP. PROB. 653, at 657 (1964).
[26] Pub. L. No. 467, 88th Cong., 2d Sess., 78 STAT. 565 (Aug. 20, 1964).

more reliable and informative quotations in the over-the-counter market.

Furthermore, the industry made substantial progress in improving itself. It tightened management controls, for example, and emphasized training of its salesmen. As soon as the Commission began asking questions, the financial community became aware of evident deficiencies. Indeed it might be said to have made its own special study. Our criticism was not met with enthusiasm, but a constructive attitude rather than total antagonism has been preserved, thanks in part to a sustained effort made to maintain thoroughness, fairness, and responsibility. As the *London Economist* said of the Study: [27] "Americans who have long admired the quality of investigations conducted by the British Royal Commission may take heart. It can happen here."

Perhaps another reason why a study of this type can have an impact upon both the commission and the industry it regulates is that there was a conscious decision to give the study group independence. It would have been impossible to secure complete agreement of all five commissioners on a 3,000 page analysis within the limited time period which we were allowed. It is obvious, moreover, that objective views can provide a new and welcome stimulus to us on the inside. Sensitive to congressional criticism, we all tend to justify every action rather than admit human, and—even more—institutional, fallibility.

Furthermore, the Commission would be required to act subsequently on the recommendations of the Report of the Special Study under the Administrative Procedure Act; and if a firm and hardened position were taken by the Commission rather than by an independent group, it would be difficult if not impossible for us to deal with the industry. Finally, it was anticipated that while the report would focus on the shortcomings in the industry and in the self-regulatory agencies, in certain respects there would be express or implied criticism of the Commission itself. Institutions, whether government, quasi-government, or private, all benefit from examination. A spirit of independence provides the addi-

---

[27] 208 London Economist 587 (1963).

tional advantage of staff enthusiasm and *esprit de corps,* coupled with a fresh point of view.

Some evidence of the give-and-take between the Commission and young staff members is the parody written after the publication of our first letter to Congress transmitting the first segment of the Report of the Special Study of Securities Markets.

The first major paragraph of the transmittal letter [28] and the take-off are set forth side by side.

Sir:

I have the honor to transmit the first segment of the Report of the Special Study of Securities Markets. . . .

At the outset we emphasize that, although many specific recommendations for improvements in rules and practices are made in the Report of the Special Study, the report demonstrates that neither the fundamental structure of the securities markets nor of the regulatory pattern of the securities acts requires dramatic reconstruction. The report should not impair public confidence in the securities markets, but should strengthen it as suggestions for raising standards are put into practice. Serious shortcomings are apparent and the report, of course, has concentrated on their examination and analysis. Yet it is not a picture of pervasive fraudulent activity and in this respect contrasts markedly with the hearings and findings of

Sir:

I have the honor to transmit the first segment of the Old Testament. This first segment includes the first five chapters starting with Exodus and is referred to as the Torah.

At the outset we emphasize that, although ten specific recommendations for improvements in rules and practices are made, the Torah demonstrates that neither the fundamental structure of society nor of the tribal chiefs requires dramatic reconstruction. . . .

The Torah should not impair public confidence in society, but should strengthen it as suggestions for raising standards are put into practice. Serious shortcomings are apparent (see Chapter III on Sodom and Gomorrah) and the Torah, of course, has concentrated on their examination and analysis. Yet it is not a picture of pervasive sinful activity and in this respect contrasts

---

[28] *Special Study,* pt. 1, p. III.

77

the early thirties preceding the enactment of the Federal securities laws. The study confirms the strength of those laws and the heightened sense of obligation of the financial community.

markedly with the reign of Genghis Khan.

At the same time the Torah makes clear that important problems do exist, grave abuses do occur, and additional improvements are needed. To assist us in carrying out such improvements, we have asked for the cooperation of a committee of Philistines. As Noah remarked, "What are a few drops of rain?"

The above may well be a criticism of the Commission as too conservative in its conclusions, or of the staff as evangelistic, as young men should be. Yet any final conclusion must be weighed in the light of the final goals which the Special Study and the Commission sought to achieve legislatively and substantively.

The pattern of the Special Study might well be applicable to other administrative agencies. On the one hand, it is desirable to introduce outsiders. In our case, the Special Study was staffed by many lawyers from private practice, economists, and university professors. On the other hand, it must not be wholly divorced from those who will have the responsibility of running the agency. There were a number from the Commission's regular staff to provide some continuity between the two stages, making recommendations and putting them into effect.

Broad surveys may well be one way of giving an agency the opportunity to turn away from its day-to-day responsibilities and ask where it is heading in the light of industry developments. These surveys are not a unique achievement of one commission. It is true that such studies have preceded and sparked many of the major reforms adopted by the SEC. In a number of instances, the requirement has been written into legislation, such as section 11(e) of the Securities Exchange Act, which directed the Commission to study the feasibility of separating the functions of dealer and broker, and report by January, 1936. In addition, section 19(c) called for a study of the rules of national securities exchanges; section 28 of the Securities Act, for a study of protective and reorganization committees; and section 30 of the Public Utility Holding Company Act of 1935 authorized the Commission to make a survey of the functions and activities of investment companies. According to Professor Sidney M. Robbins, "To prevent the laxness that might otherwise set in with age and the tendency for a commission to learn to live in amiable comfort with the regulated industry, the Securities Exchange Act might be amended to require a special study periodically to serve as a soul-searching review of the effectiveness of regulations and the adequacy of existing standards." [29] To some extent his suggestion is already incorporated in the Securities Acts Amendments of 1964 (sec. 20(c) of the Securities Exchange Act of 1934, as amended), already referred to in Chapter 2; Conclusion, page 59.

The FPC followed a similar pattern in its long-term study of the nation's future electric power needs entitled "National Power Survey" and submitted to Congress in 1964. Whether or not one agrees with its conclusions, it provided a basis for considering the impact of the blackout in the northeastern United States on November 9, 1965, attributed to the present system of power interconnections. The FCC has likewise commissioned outside studies of major problems with which it is faced, such as the Barrow Report of 1958 on broadcasting. The Landis Report cites others.[30]

This pattern among agencies is certainly to be encouraged. It is a means not only of concentrating on the major policy problems of the agency and exploring the shifts and changes in the industry to be regulated, and of obtaining a needed increase in budget and an infusion of new blood, but it also faces Congress with something concrete that it should consider.

*Investment Company Surveys.* Another approach to reexamination of the Commission's role concentrated on the Investment Company Act of 1940. It had its genesis more than eight years ago, in 1958. The industry has gone through dynamic changes, and there is some question whether the act has the plasticity to

---

[29] S Robbins, The Securities Markets: Operations and Issues, p. 77 (Free Press, 1966).

[30] *Landis Report,* p. 18.

79

meet them. Until recently the Commission's administration of the Investment Company Act was largely focused on disclosure requirements, occasional enforcement of regulatory provisions, and many intellectually difficult problems involving exemptions.

Only in the late fifties did the SEC fully appreciate that this was no longer a modest industry whose relative insignificance in comparison with other investment media had tended to obscure basic questions warranting thorough examination. Lately the industry had become a major alternative among investors' choices. Investment companies had grown from 2.5 billion dollars in 1940 to over 23 billion in 1960 and 36 billion in 1963.[31] Shareholder accounts of mutual funds were 296 thousand in 1940, 4.9 million in 1960, and over 6 million in 1963.[32] Furthermore, administration of the act could no longer be confined to the traditional investment company alone. Other financial institutions developed means to take advantage of the mutual fund concept which was attracting public funds, first the insurance companies with variable annuities, and now the banks with variations of their traditional common trust funds. In consequence, a new approach was sought upon which to base regulation of both the variable annuities of insurance companies and the commingled accounts of banks, without impinging on the traditional jurisdiction of insurance or banking regulatory authorities. As stated in Chapter 2, our position was that these institutions were moving squarely into the mutual fund business, and hence that all investors in mutual funds should receive the same protections, regardless of whether the fund was sponsored by a bank,[33] an insurance company,[34] a broker, an investment counselor, or any other person. Ultimately, the leading bank protagonist, the First National City Bank of

---

[31] SEC, CLASSIFICATION, ASSETS AND TAXATION OF REGISTERED INVESTMENT COMPANIES UNDER THE 1940 ACT AS OF JUNE 30, 1963.

[32] WIESENBERGER, INVESTMENT COMPANIES 28 (1963).

[33] Letter to Senator Robertson, 109 CONG. REC. 25187–25189 (Dec. 19, 1963); *Hearing on Common Trust Funds Before a Subcommittee of the House Committee on Government Operations,* 88th Cong., 1st Sess. (May 20, 1963), pp. 3ff.

[34] *Securities and Exchange Comm'n v. Variable Annuity Life Ins. Co.,* 359 U.S. 65 (1959); The Prudential Insurance Company of America, SEC Investment Co. Act Release No. 3620, Jan. 22, 1963, *aff'd, Prudential Ins. Co. v. SEC,* 326 F.2d 383 (3d Cir. 1964).

New York, accepted this principle and took steps to register the commingled fund that it proposed to establish.[35]

Again, as a fresh approach both to the understanding by investment companies of the basic requirements of the 1940 act and to its more effective enforcement, we developed a new comprehensive annual report form to be certified by the fund's independent certified public accountant.[36] This represents a move toward self-inspection which is consistent with a philosophy that part of the regulatory responsibility should be placed upon the industry. There is no reason why government should expand when others can be induced to fill the vacuum.[37]

In an attempt to resolve the structural problems inherent in the investment company industry, we were fortunate in having already underway, since 1958, a study of mutual funds prepared for the Commission by the Wharton School of Finance and Commerce. It was made public in 1962.[38] This was supplemented, particularly as to the selling area, by work of the Special Study,[39] and, as to the industry structure, by extensive case studies by a group brought especially to the Commission and operating within the permanent staff. We examined the highly competitive drive to sell mutual funds and the devices used for that purpose, such as contractual or front-end load plans.[40] In many instances, these plans involve a commission of 50 percent of the first year's payment, which may be lost if the contract lapses (known as the front-end load). Without our taking direct action (since it would probably require statutory amendment), the very study of the field resulted in a trend to voluntary reduction of its impact by lessening and stretching out the load.[41]

---

[35] See In the Matter of First National City Bank, Investment Co. Act Release No. 4538 (Mar. 9, 1966).

[36] See speech by William L. Cary, "The Securities and Exchange Commission After the Special Study of Securities Markets," Investment Bankers Association of America, Dec. 3, 1963. It was adopted Jan. 25, 1965 as Form N-1R.

[37] Cary, Self-Regulation in the Securities Industry, 49 A.B.A.J. 244, 247 (1963).

[38] A Study of Mutual Funds, H.R. REP. No. 2274, 87th Cong., 2d Sess. (1962).

[39] Special Study, pt. 4, ch. XI.

[40] Id. at 172.

[41] Registration Statement No. 2–15015, Variable Annuity Life Ins. Co., post effective amendment filed with SEC April 7, 1964. "Investors Diversified Services, the biggest of the mutual-fund organizations, began selling such a

Through our studies, also, we came to identify the consequences of conflicts of interest fostered by the nature of the industry structure, and tolerated within the act. In analyzing investment companies we found a number of potential or actual problems which are inherent in the present pattern of the industry. Many of them stem from a unique historical development, for the management of investment funds has been primarily by contract with outsiders rather than by employees of the company itself. In part as a result of our activities and in part because of some sixty odd lawsuits brought by complaining shareholders, there is some evidence that the fund directors are now increasingly aware of their responsibility and are assuming more active and vigorous roles. However, in arriving at any totally satisfactory solution, a new investment company act might be required [42] and, politically, might require as much effort as was expended on the Securities Acts Amendments of 1964 to be discussed in the next chapter.

*Adjudication.* Another fruitful avenue to development within the agency can be through the process of adjudication. Sometimes more can be achieved by the approach of the common law, i.e., by accretion, than by a rule. In fact, only thus may it be possible to etch out a policy which can be adequately tested through experience. In a recent article my successor,[43] Manuel F. Cohen, has demonstrated the importance of adjudication in the development of standards for broker-dealers under the antifraud provisions of the securities laws. The infinite variety of fraud and the ease of evading specific rules has made necessary reliance on adjudication in this vital area.

By way of illustration, *In the Matter of Cady Roberts & Co.*[44] indicates the flexibility provided by adjudication, as well as the value of dealing with a concrete factual situation. That case,

---

'spread-load' plan last fall." N.Y. Times, May 16, 1966, p. 1, col. 4; also p. 55, col. 4.

[42] See N.Y. Times, May 16, 1966, p. 55, col. 1.

[43] Cohen & Rabin, *Broker-Dealer Selling Practice Standards: The Importance of Administrative Adjudication in Their Development,* 29 LAW & CONTEMP. PROB. 691 (1964).

[44] 40 SEC 907 (1961).

stated broadly, concerned the duties of all persons possessing nonpublic information as a result of a special relationship with an issuer of securities, but specifically dealt with the duties of a broker-dealer. He had executed sales on an exchange for his discretionary accounts because of his knowledge of a dividend reduction not yet publicly announced, which he received from a director associated with his brokerage firm. The Commission held that because of the broker's special access to corporate information and the unfairness of executing the sales before the information became public, his conduct violated the antifraud provisions. Under the circumstances, the SEC indicated that if disclosure was not practicable, the proper course would have been to forgo the transaction until news of the dividend reduction had been announced.

As Mr. Cohen has pointed out, this case has significance because it applies the high standards required of corporate insiders to a person who received his information from an insider with whom he was associated, and because it applies to sales on an exchange, where he made no representations and, in fact, had no actual contact with the purchaser. There is, at least, a reasonable question whether the Commission would or even could have promulgated a general formal rule embodying the standard of conduct initiated in this case without an actual situation before it. It would be a never-ending task to attempt to draft a series of rules each having a specific and limited application, and it would be virtually impossible to reach the myriad situations which could arise.*

Professor Kenneth C. Davis in his excellent treatise has raised the question whether the *Cady, Roberts* and like opinions could not be accomplished as well or better in a rule.[45] A rule has the value of being published and subjected to public comment and

---

* There may appear to be an element of unfairness in setting a new course at the expense of a particular defendant. In recognition of this problem, it has been the Commission's custom to apply leniency in the sanction if the policy decision is one of first impression. In fact, one commissioner dissented in Cady Roberts & Company because the "facts and violations require the imposition of a greater sanction" (40 S.E.C. at 918).

[45] Davis, Administrative Law Treatise, § 6.13, p. 146 (Supp. 1965) [hereafter referred to as Davis].

industry criticism. The decision in *Cady, Roberts* was in fact broadly criticized when it was promulgated. At that time I received a telephone call from the president of the New York Stock Exchange, who read to me a strongly critical letter he was about to send characterizing this as an unwarranted step toward raising standards to an unrealistic level. The letter was never in fact received, and the New York Stock Exchange instead issued an excellent set of directives to its member firms which carried forward some of the principles enunciated in this case.[46]

Yet the decision itself leaves open many questions. Does it apply to persons other than broker-dealers? What is material information? Who are insiders? How long should an insider refrain from trading? How far do the sanctions extend, and to what extent is there liability to private persons? All these can be gradually developed through succeeding opinions. Indeed, some of them are before the courts, in the case of *SEC v. Texas Gulf Sulphur Company et al.*[47] I share Professor Davis' emphasis on rule making: all the agencies should be enunciating policy much more by this route. Yet I do not believe it must be relied upon exclusively. A combination of administrative and court proceedings can also perform a proper role in developing (or, if necessary, delimiting) a policy that the Commission has sponsored. At the same time, this affords all the protections of the judicial process.

In the foregoing it should be emphasized that we are concerned only with formal adjudication and commission opinions, not with the great bulk of the business of the SEC and other federal agencies. The actual number of formal SEC opinions after hearing and upon the basis of a record is relatively small. In 1963, according to Professor Davis,[48] they were 175, as compared with 1157 registration statements and some 30,000 advisory letters. Even among these 175, many were routine broker-dealer revocation proceedings. After the hearing these cases are discussed and debated within the Commission, in the presence of lawyers from the Office of Opinions and Review, one or more of whom are assigned to prepare a draft. They provide both continuity and pains-

---

[46] N.Y. Stk. Exch. Educational Circular No. 151 (Dec. 15, 1961).

[47] Civil No. 1182/1965, S.D.N.Y., complaint filed April 19, 1965.

[48] DAVIS, *op. cit.*, § 1.02, p. 11 (Supp. 1965).

taking study of the record. In his 1960 report Mr. Landis recommended that the opinion writing section be abolished,[49] and that "Commissioners [be] held individually responsible for the enunciation of the grounds upon which conclusions of the Commission are stated to rest." I do not believe this is a proper allocation of time unless the case is blazing a new path or is otherwise significant.

Here again delegation is appropriate to keep the attention of the Commission constantly focused upon the essentials: i.e., important decisions, rule making, and reexamination of policy in the light of changing industry patterns. The SEC has taken significant steps to delegate responsibility under new congressional authority.[50] Now many administrative decisions not involving novel or important questions are being made by the heads of its operating divisions with a right of appeal to the Commission by the persons adversely affected.[51] In the area of adjudication greater authority has been given to the staff of hearing examiners and to the Office of Opinions and Review. Review by the Commission has been limited by a type of certiorari and summary affirmance procedure to cases involving important questions of law or policy or in which there have been materially erroneous findings of fact or conclusions of law.[52] Even more delegation might be appropriate, if the pressure of business should ever require, which is not the case now. The Commission could establish then a board of review composed of senior staff members acting independently of the operating divisions. This kind of board, limited to adjudicatory matters, was set up by the Federal Communications Commission in 1962,[53] and it is said to be working well.

The cost of delegation is not too great. True, the Commission itself will not be able to attend to every detail or parse every sen-

---

[49] *Landis Report,* p. 47.
[50] 76 STAT. 394 (1962), 15 U.S.C. § 78d-1 (Supp. IV, 1963).
[51] See Arts. 30-1 to 30-5, SEC Statement of Organization, Conduct, Ethics and Information Practices, 17 C.F.R. §§ 200.30-1 to 200.30-5.
[52] See Arts. 30-6 to 30-7, SEC Statement of Organization, Conduct, Ethics and Information Practices, 29 FED. REG. 9486–9490 (July 11, 1964); SEC Securities Act Releases Nos. 4704 and 4705 (June 30, 1964).
[53] See FCC 62–612, 27 FED. REG. 5671 (June 14, 1962), following enactment of Pub. L. 87–192, 75 STAT. 420 (Aug. 31, 1961).

tence, but under a system of delegated authority, responsibility will not be fragmented, and important matters, whether they arise administratively, legislatively, or in the adjudication of particular cases, will still be handled by those who have overall regulatory experience and responsibility.*

## Personnel and Funds

Hand in hand with the program of reexamination was the effort of getting and keeping good people. It is impossible to make headway without the zeal of a devoted staff combined with independent views from the outside. This problem—personnel— is an ever-present one in government, particularly when the agency is not attempting to move ahead but simply to carry on its day-to-day responsibilities. As already indicated, the Commission

---

* Other areas for restudy still present themselves to the SEC for the future. One is the field of disclosure, involving the registration statements and proxy statements, in which the Commission has done a thorough job and developed a commendable tradition. The Report of the Special Study indicated that "the Commission's administration of the registration provisions of the Securities Act has been one of its most outstanding achievements and the statute itself has proved generally adequate and workable." Yet on a longer-term basis, efforts should be made to achieve a greater integration as to information required under the Securities Act of 1933 and the Securities Exchange Act of 1934. There is substantial question whether companies supplying information currently should be subjected to another and more complete registration process every time they go to the market for funds. It should be recognized that most financing by corporations today is through debt or self-generated funds; hence, the principal medium of public investment is not in new issues but in the trading of stocks presently outstanding or investing through institutions, such as pension trusts, mutual funds, or insurance companies. This, therefore, should be the principal focus for the protection of investors.

The Special Study also has pointed to an expanding area for further investigation, much of it focused around the application of the antitrust laws. Since 1963, particularly since the decision of the Supreme Court in *Silver v. New York Stock Exchange*, 373 U.S. 341 (1963) suits have been filed and questions raised about the principle of the fixed commission rate schedule for securities traded on the exchanges, the absence of a volume discount, the correlative development of a third market, i.e., the trading of listed securities off the exchange, and the growth of regional exchanges to deal in dually listed securities. All these point to dramatic changes in the securities markets during the next decade.

has had a tradition and a reserve of excellent, able, and dedicated public servants. Yet when I came to the SEC, I was told by people on the staff not to try to get any new top-ranking law graduates and young lawyers, first because we could not attract them, and second because they would leave. These are premises with which I totally disagree. We strove to demonstrate the error of the first point, to bring again to the Commission the reputation it enjoyed in the 1930s, when almost every young lawyer in the government wanted to be associated with the SEC. In this effort we had some success. We also found by statistical analysis that superior lawyers generally leave the SEC no sooner and no later than average ones. Much depends on whether their efforts are recognized and their talents fully challenged. Happily, our long tradition of intellectual insubordination (encouraging everyone to speak his mind) has continued to flourish, and this in turn has kindled excitement in the work. It is often wanting in government institutions.

Morale can decline as readily as it can rise. To a large extent it is a function of the chairman, and whether the agency is moving ahead or settling back into routine administration. On some occasions the appointment of a single commissioner can effect a change of attitude. When the announcement was made of President Johnson's decision to fill the first vacancy on the SEC with a man who was sponsored by the Republican minority leader, and whom rumor erroneously described as opposed to all government regulation, there was a noticeable flurry among some of the ablest young lawyers. They wanted to know whether the time had come to look around for outside opportunities. And they had to be assured that the allegations were not true, and that the appointment did not represent a reversal of policy upon the part of the new administration.

It must be recognized that the personnel problem is in part a function of the budget, as reflected in salaries, promotions, and the opportunity to bring in new and able young people, particularly lawyers. Here again, the effort to introduce new thinking may in turn generate encouragement from the Bureau of the Budget, the Civil Service Commission (as to supergrades), and from Congress. To some extent there is a circular effect; a larger budget enables an agency to look ahead of its day-to-day responsibilities, while if it looks ahead, Congress and the executive may find a basis for making more funds available. In this respect the Commission has had good fortune with an increase in budget over four years from $9.5 million for 1961 to $15.4 million for 1965, and in personnel from 1,090 to 1,462.[54] The move to expand within limits is, I trust, to be differentiated from "empire building": a common hallmark of business as well as government administration. We were not interested in growth as such. Indeed we firmly declined suggestions by members of Congress that we undertake new tasks not directly related to securities regulation, such as the reporting of investments under the Federal Welfare and Pension Plans Disclosure Act (administered by the Department of Labor), or the proposal made in an editorial of the *New York Times* that we make a study of the commodity exchanges after the salad oil scandal of 1963.[55]

## Conclusion

In conclusion, I do not believe that *rigor mortis* is necessarily the lot of every commission, or that an agency is incapable of resuscitation. Yet I recognize that enormous obstacles stand in the way of maintaining vitality. A conjunction of events and fresh ideas, and luck, resulting in congressional response and a budgetary increase, are necessary prerequisites to avoiding inertia, or perhaps the fate envisioned by Galbraith. I further believe that the SEC has probably sustained its vitality over the years more than its sister agencies, and that this is due in no small part to the fact that it kept having new statutes to administer or was seeking legislation to meet new problems.

I do not wish to imply that experience recounted here as to the SEC is fully applicable across the board. It is undoubtedly necessary to distinguish between agencies which operate under the cloak of a general consensus and those which do not. The basic aim of securities legislation is to develop an informed market and minimize the amount of fraud and dishonesty in it. For such an end one can sustain a crusade. On occasion this may be equally

---

[54] SEC ANN. REP. 30, p. 161 (1964).
[55] Editorial, "The Soybean Mystery," N.Y. Times, Dec. 12, 1963.

true as to the FTC. No such consensus applies to agencies like the CAB, ICC, FCC, and FPC. The first two were developed by legislative design to protect the industry and, particularly in the case of the CAB, to promote it. This does not lend itself to any reform movement. Controversy arises when the industry is divided into segments, as, for example, rail, water, and motor carriers under the ICC, and one mode of transportation seeks to thwart another. In the case of the FPC, it should be recognized that natural gas producer regulation (as distinguished from pipeline regulation) came about as a judicial accident out of the *Phillips* [56] case, while the FCC has a statute formulated primarily in response to the problem of electronic interference. Congress never expressly considered the economics of either industry or the impact of the public interest in any concrete or clear form. As a consequence, these four agencies might have more trouble than the SEC in exercising initiative. Still, every program of reexamination and policy planning need not take the form of a crusade.

---

[56] *Phillips Petroleum Co. v. Wisconsin,* 347 U.S. 672 (1954).

# 4 | *Shepherding an Agency-*

## *sponsored Bill through Congress*

To many lawmakers on Capitol Hill nothing is more unsettling than the prospect of making a law—at any rate, a law involving the least trace of controversy. The passage of almost any piece of legislation is bound to offend someone, and in politics it is not so much the good will of one's friends that counts as the wrath of one's enemies.—From THE REAL VOICE by Richard Harris

The business of amendment or alteration of lawes is a choice and tender business, neither wholly to be omitted when the necessity requires, and yet very cautiously and warily to be undertaken, though the necessity may, or, at least, may seem to require it.— From CONSIDERATIONS TOUCHING THE AMENDMENT OR ALTERATION OF LAWES by Lord Chief Justice Sir Matthew Hale

### Introduction

This is the history of a nonsponsored bill, sought by the agency but having no identifiable partisan in the House or Senate. It could also be described as a "noncontroversial" bill, a reform measure which we thought no one could possibly oppose. Having been through the trauma of trying to get a noncontroversial bill passed, I now wonder what more could happen if one had dealt with a controversial one. It required patience, persistence, persuasion, a high boiling point, and, finally, a great deal of luck.

The Securities Act Amendments of 1964 [1] was of major significance to the SEC. It included provisions for which the Commission had been yearning over eighteen years. On the scale of political values, the bill was of medium or perhaps minor importance. The primary responsibility for pushing it rested with the SEC. The bill in some cases enjoyed support, or at least acquiescence, from Republicans as well as Democrats and from conservatives as well as from liberals. Yet the obstacles faced by the Commission in obtaining passage of this bill demonstrate the difficulties of obtaining from Congress any reform legislation where there is no special economic benefit to any congressional group, as well as the persistence and tenacity needed even in an almost ideal climate such as ours enjoyed.

The bill can be said to consist of two main parts: The first and perhaps most important had been before Congress in different forms three times since 1946, the high tide being a favorable report by the Senate Banking and Currency Committee in 1957.[2] It involved the application of certain investor protections [*] to the

---

[1] Pub. L. 88–467, 88th Cong., 2d Sess., S. 1642 (Aug. 20, 1964).

[2] S. Rep. No. 700, 85th Cong., 1st Sess. (1957).

[*] Specifically these protections are:

1) The application of registration requirements imposing the duty upon the company to disclose all material information regarding its business together with financial statements; and to keep the information current by periodic reports.

2) The application of the proxy rules. Up to 1955 they were aimed primarily at regulating the solicitation of proxies on the part of management. First of all they seek disclosure to the shareholders of all material relevant to proposals for corporate action (including election of directors). Second, the use of fraud is made unlawful in the solicitation of proxies. Third, opportunity is afforded to stockholders themselves to solicit proxies, and to make proposals to their fellow shareholders. After 1955, the proxy provisions were made applicable also to outsiders seeking control in proxy contests.

3) The application of the insider trading provisions (i.e., Section 16) to corporate directors, officers, and principal shareholders. It is designed to protect the outside shareholders against short-swing speculation by

securities of all companies having more than 750 shareholders (later to be reduced to 500 shareholders), and 1 million dollars in assets. These protections hitherto had applied only to listed concerns but were to be extended by carrying forward the disclosure policy, and discouraging short-swing profits by insiders to all companies which may fairly be considered in public hands. This I shall refer to as the corporate segment of the bill.

The second part relates primarily to raising the qualifications of persons in the industry, particularly broker-dealers. It enacts higher standards for persons entering the industry and broader disciplinary controls over them. This part I shall refer to as the broker-dealer segment of the bill. The bill would never have been passed, indeed it would never have been seriously considered, had it not been for the Special Study of the Securities Markets, authorized by Congress in 1961 and completed on August 8, 1963, and the momentum that it provided.

## The Special Study

The contents of the Special Study have already been discussed in another context (Chapter 3) and hence need not be repeated here. Nevertheless, there should be no illusion that an appropriation for such a study requires a minimum of effort. Two steps must always be taken: first the authorization, and then the appropriation. On the original authorization there were hearings before the House committee of substantial length, demonstrating the condition of the market in 1960 and 1961,[3] and again hearings before a House subcommittee in connection with the original appropriation of $750,000. At this point, we did have a sponsor in Congressman Peter Mack of Illinois (defeated in 1962), and the help of Congressman Albert Thomas, a powerful appropriations subcommittee chairman who was generally sympathetic to the

---

insiders. The latter are required to report changes in their share ownership, and are subject to liability for any profit from any purchases and sales, or sales and purchases, of equity securities, within a six-month period.

[3] *Hearings before a Subcommittee of the House Committee on Interstate and Foreign Commerce* [hereafter referred to as *House Hearings*], 87th Cong., 1st Sess. on H.R.J. Res. 438 [Securities Markets Investigation], June 27, 28, 29 and July 10, 1961.

work we were doing. Though there was a hearing before the Senate committee, the Senate accepted the House action without hesitation.[4]

When we found that our project took longer than we had anticipated and required more funds, we had again to return to Congress to obtain an extension of time in the form of a new authorization and go through all the appropriate channels again for an additional sum of $200,000.[5] The latter effort was arduous but totally in vain, for after proceeding through the House and working valiantly to get our appropriation into the bill for 1962, there was a dispute over protocol between the chairmen of the Appropriations Committee of the Senate and of the House and on the final night of the session the omnibus appropriations bill was not voted upon and died. For this reason the extra funds necessary to complete the study had to be squeezed out of our day-to-day budget with considerable strain.

Upon completion of the first segment of the Special Study on April 3, 1963,[6] as required by statute, the initial set of hearings upon our report immediately got under way. As already noted in the preceding chapter, we had made a decision that the Study should be the product of a group known as the Special Study of the Securities Market, not the product of the Commission, although we worked very closely with the study group, and had examined each part of their work and made our comments. This proved a wise judgment, for five independently minded commissioners would have difficulty in reaching recommendations without frequent dissents or alternative suggestions. It was indeed the only way to get before the public a thorough presentation of the existing status of the securities market within the deadline prescribed. In transmitting the first segment we did provide in broad outline the legislative program that we would propose based

---

[4] H.R.J. Res. 438 was approved Sept. 5, 1961 as Pub. L. 87–196, 87th Cong. as an amendment (subsection (d)) to Section 19 of the Securities Exchange Act of 1934.
[5] Pub. L. 87–561, 87th Cong., H.R. 11670, July 27, 1963: amending section 19(d) above, by changing Jan. 3, 1963 to April 3, and increasing the $750,000 figure to $950,000.
[6] *Special Study*, pts. 1 and 3 were submitted on April 3.

upon the findings in the Study. Yet as soon as we appeared before Congress, Congressman Dingell, who was a friend, nevertheless took sharp issue with us, pointing to the direction in the statute that the "Commission shall report" to the Congress and claiming that we were avoiding our responsibility. He said: [7] "I am quite an admirer of yours. [Note the lull before the storm.] . . . You say this is a report of the Commission and yet you say it is not a report of the Commission. By statute you are to bring us the report of the Commission and not a report of a group within the Commission which is in effect reporting to the Commission, which, in turn transmits this matter to the Congress without endorsement of the Commission of the principles and statements therein." The capacity to take criticism is a necessary ingredient of any public servant. In this case, it was not a burden because the chairman and committee members did praise the careful and responsible work that had been done, though indicating weaknesses which they believed to exist. Mr. Dingell's criticism, moreover, was not without merit.

An atmosphere of rapport can quickly change into an abrasive one, but we arrived at a formula with the help of Chairman Harris which would satisfy both Congress and the Commission. In answer to a letter from him, we replied on April 19 and specifically gave our views with respect to each of the recommendations made in the first segment of the Special Study.[8] It was a good example of the political skill of a chairman seeking to satisfy both sides.

The first part of the Study of the Securities Markets was widely anticipated by the press and thoroughly covered on the front pages.[9] There was much apprehension on the part of the industry and considerable criticism of our conclusions with respect to the existence of fraud. At the same time, the financial community was keenly aware of the fact that we had exercised a high degree of restraint and responsibility in our report and comments in the letter of transmittal. As already noted, some of the evangelists of the

---

[7] *House Hearings*, 88th Cong., 1st Sess. on H.R. 6789, H.R. 6793, S. 1642, April 3, 1963 (pt. 1, Investor Protection), p. 10.

[8] *Ibid.*, p. 28.

[9] See N.Y. Times, April 4, 1963, p. 1, col. 8; p. 42 (entire).

staff considered our letter too mild, and wrote a parody upon it (see Chapter 3; Possible Approaches, page 77).

## Negotiating the Bill

In the days immediately preceding the publication of our first report, we concluded that before submitting a bill to Congress, it should be first discussed with representatives of the industry. Even with the momentum created by the Study, it seemed advisable to achieve the maximum possible agreement in the financial community before we reached Congress, both on policy and technical detail. As noted in Chapter 3, in the light of the history of securities legislation I think it can be fairly said that it is impossible, or at least unlikely (except in moments of public outrage) for a bill to be acceptable to Congress to which all the industry strongly objects.

As a general rule, meeting with groups which are not in favor of a bill or with members of Congress who oppose it is highly advisable. For example, we did not gain support from the National Association of Manufacturers,[10] but in talking with them were able to demonstrate that ours was not a regulatory agency grasping for power but one which had a rational basis for expanding disclosure by publicly owned companies to increase investor confidence, and "make capitalism work." Thus, at least we blunted the opposition. With the United States Chamber of Commerce, our success was greater; having objected to legislation in earlier years, the Chamber ultimately supported part of our bill this time.[11]

As soon as we had transmitted the first part of the Special Study to Congress, we sent identical letters to the leaders of the securities industry, asking them to form a liaison group to work

---

[10] See letter of W. P. Gullander, President, NAM, dated Nov. 27, 1964. *House Hearings* [Part 2, Investor Protection], p. 1415.

[11] The United States Chamber of Commerce supported the corporate segment of the bill, but urged the exemption of insurance companies. See letter dated July 2, 1963, *Hearings before a Subcommittee of the Senate Committee on Banking and Currency*, 88th Cong., 1st Sess. on S. 1642 [SEC Legislation, 1963], p. 277; compare its attitude before the same committee in 1957, *Senate Hearings*, 85th Cong., 1st Sess. [SEC Legislation], p. 259.

with us on legislation.[12] It came to be known as the Industry Liaison Committee. There was considerable hesitation, and tension, in the first conference on April 19, for they felt that they could not bind their organizations. We gave them a short deadline because Chairman Harris had told us the bill should be filed by July 1. But when they demonstrated it was impossible, we wanted to show a united front and went back to him with Amyas Ames, the able head of the Investment Bankers Association, and obtained an extension which they believed was feasible if they could muster their groups swiftly, which indeed they did.

There were three major points to which the industry objected and on which we yielded. First of all, there was a question about the so-called market makers—dealers who stand ready to buy and sell a company's stock. In the over-the-counter market, these are the key to liquidity. By definition there is no exchange to which buy and sell orders flow; the market makers perform that function. The basic question was whether persons who might have underwritten the initial public issue and might be serving on the board, and who presently make a market in the company's shares as the principal buyer and seller should be subject to the short-swing "insider" trading provisions of Section 16(b). As earlier noted, this subjects directors, officers, and principal shareholders to liability for any profit made in purchasing and selling, or selling and purchasing the company's stock within a six-month period. Some of the most reputable men in the industry had always disagreed with our position and claimed that in a small business going to the public for funds the sponsors of an issue assume some responsibility for its success and for maintaining a market over the counter; and that a short-swing trading sanction applicable to directors would halt their dealing in the company's shares and would hence be detrimental to it. This was a position on which we were not persuaded. Our Special Study [13] had presented strong evidence to the contrary, yet it was strongly held by the reliable spokesmen for the industry and seemed to be one which we could give up. At a later time we were to be accused by

---

[12] Letter dated April 3, 1963 to Messrs. Lemkau, Ames, and Funston, *House Hearings* [pt. 1, Investor Protection], p. 650.
[13] *Special Study*, pt. 3, at p. 47.

a liberal Congressman of having made a "contract" with the industry when he urged us to put it back into the bill. Perhaps he was right, but perhaps we were right to concede.

The second was a proposed amendment, [entitled 15(a)(k) (2)] which would have given the Commission powers to change the rules of the National Association of Securities Dealers comparable to those which we exercised over the exchanges. This was a logical sequence, but since they would not support it and demonstrated that the NASD had never taken issue with us once our position with respect to a rule was clear, we dropped the proposal.

Finally, the industry fought against application of the bill to foreign securities and we framed the provision in such a way that in effect all foreign securities would be exempted initially, but exemption would be subject to review upon notice, hearing, and order of the Commission.[14]

Quite apart from the general political climate and the shortcomings noted in the Special Study (see Chapter 3) there were other factors responsible for the generally statesmanlike attitude on the part of the industry. It was represented by some high-grade and broad-minded leaders. Our constant theme, often repeated in speeches and discussion, was that we were attempting to lift the standards of the industry to the level of the responsible people within it. They recognized that standards were deficient and should be improved. Yet there was also a good measure of self-interest: at least the exchanges and the member firms would benefit substantially from the application of the first, or corporate, segment of the act to widely held companies trading over the counter. They had not previously been subject to any disclosure, proxy, or insider trading requirements so long as they remained unlisted. But now this inducement to refrain from listing would disappear. Thus the exchanges and the major broker-dealers had expectations of more listings and more business, and supported the bill.

At a later date some of our liberal friends were to raise a ques-

---

[14] As will be developed, this provision was revised by the House to include foreign issuers but to give the Commission authority to exempt them. See Sec. 12(g)(3) of the Securities Exchange Act, as amended.

tion about the concurrence obtained. One congressman said: "Why, there isn't a single provision opposed by the industry." Yet he failed to add that if there had been strong objection the bill might not even have received a hearing. Furthermore, there comes a time when the points of opposition, even on technical matters, become so numerous that a committee will lose interest in salvaging the residue on which there is agreement. In agreeing upon a bill, one further understanding was reached of the utmost importance: namely, that since the Commission would be engaged in implementing recommendations of the Special Study through its rule making powers, any controversy generated over rule proposals would not carry over and jeopardize the accord already reached as to the bill itself.

### Drafting Considerations

In offering legislation, there is always the basic question whether two separate proposals should be linked in a single bill, or whether they should be separate. Chairman Harris pointed out the alternatives: if we were more worried about one than another, it might be advisable to tie them together. Such indeed was the case, because there was not so much active support for the broker-dealer provisions as for the corporate ones. For this reason we decided upon a single bill for submission to Congress.

As to the kind of bill to be submitted, it may be interesting to note different philosophies that are expressed. Congressman Mack (who was defeated in 1962) indicated his belief that an agency should not shirk from preparing a bill which it thought was necessary regardless of its political reception, for this was a matter to be left to Congress. If Congress is likely to ignore the bill or there is little hope for it, I should be inclined to agree. Yet from personal experience, I believe his view is unrealistic, for the most important feature is to prepare a bill which has sufficient appeal that the chairmen of the respective committees will be willing to hold hearings. Just as the prerequisite for a statesman is to get elected, so the first step in an agency-sponsored bill is to get a hearing.

While meeting with the industry and drafting a bill which had its general concurrence, we at the same time submitted our proposals to the Bureau of the Budget for comment. One of its roles is to ensure coordination with other agencies.* After obtaining Bureau of the Budget concurrence, we transmitted the bill to both the Senate and the House. Senator Robertson, chairman of the Banking and Currency Committee, introduced the bill in the Senate "by request," thus taking no personal responsibility for its sponsorship. Yet he agreed to hold an early hearing, and upon the first day praised our Special Study, saying (*Senate Hearings* [SEC Legislation 1963], p. 4): "I frankly cannot recall any investigation of a comparable nature and size which has been so favorably received."

In this connection, tribute must be paid to the role of chiefs of staffs for the committees, and advisers to the committee chairmen. Individual congressmen should rely upon them more than they do. Both on the Senate and House side, there were persons of great integrity, a high degree of sophistication and ability, who could not speak for their chairmen but who, once they were convinced, could have a major impact, particularly in connection with a technical bill. I firmly believe that any government official below the level of a Cabinet official cannot afford to limit his discussion of legislation in which he is interested to the congressmen and senators alone, but at some point should discuss it with these assistants, so that the staff becomes aware of the details and value of a bill which their principals are considering. In the light of pressures upon a representative's time, the "grass roots" are not only in the congressman's district, but in his own office.

### Reception in the Senate

On the Senate side, probably the major opposition which we anticipated concerned banks, and came from a government official, the Comptroller of the Currency, James J. Saxon. We had already had some difficulty with Mr. Saxon in connection with an

---

* An objection came from the Department of Justice about compulsory membership in a self-regulatory organization, to be discussed later in this chapter. Justice noted the anticompetitive effects of self-regulation and questioned the adequacy of Commission review, but agreed not to object if we made every effort to have the legislative history reflect the broad view we had always taken of our supervisory powers and responsibilities.

unrelated subject: as already indicated (Chapter 2; The Budget, pages 39–41), the SEC was taking the position that banks would have to register the interests they sell if they went into the mutual fund business and Mr. Saxon publicly attacked us, saying we were grasping for power over banks.[15]

The Comptroller's office is a one-man regulatory agency. It has the potential advantage of making policy swiftly and unequivo-cally (sometimes impetuously), avoiding negotiation and clear-ance with independent commissioners. In our case the Comptrol-ler had taken a strong position against the first segment of the bill which would impose the same disclosure and other standards upon banks as upon all industrial and insurance companies. We felt that securities holders of all publicly held concerns should re-ceive similar protection. His position was that controls were al-ready available over national banks and that he was beginning to take action much along the lines we proposed, as indeed he was.[16] However, there were no comparable controls available over large state banks subject to the supervision of the Federal Reserve Board and the Federal Deposit Insurance Corporation —almost half of the banks whose stock was widely traded. He further charged that banks were already heavily regulated, and that the SEC was another agency trying to usurp jurisdiction. In order to head off the latter objection we inserted in our bill the provision that "all powers [and] . . . duties shall be delegated to the appropriate banking regulatory authority upon its request." At the Senate hearing we were asked if the Commission would object to a provision that would vest jurisdiction directly in the respective banking agencies, and we replied that we had none.[17]

We fully recognized that there would be substantial opposition from the banks and that if they were successful in obtaining an exemption, the insurance industry would insist upon uniform

---

[15] "Saxon Urges Banks to Challenge SEC Bid to Regulate any Pooled Invest-ment Funds," Wall Street Journal, Mar. 13, 1963, p. 5, col. 2. See N.Y. Times, June 7, 1963, p. 39, col. 3, referring to Mr. Saxon's statement of June 5.

[16] Saxon testimony, Senate Hearings [SEC Legislation 1963], June 24, 1963, p. 171.

[17] Reply to Senator Javits. Senate Hearings [SEC Legislation 1963], June 18, 1963, p. 20.

treatment. This had actually happened in the SEC bill of 1957, known as the Frear Fulbright bill.[18] Since banks and insurance companies constitute the two most important industries whose shares were selling on the over-the-counter market, regardless of size, it was imperative to have them included in the corporate part of the bill. Bank stocks alone accounted for one-fifth of the securities on the over-the-counter market.[19] We recognized that the banks would make a highly effective argument against regulation by other Federal agencies than the ones presently overseeing their industry (i.e., the Comptroller of the Currency as to national banks, the Federal Reserve Board as to Reserve Member banks and the Federal Deposit Insurance Corporation as to the balance).

We already had the support of the Federal Reserve Board [20] and with the last compromise, of the American Bankers Association.[21] In fact both William MacChesney Martin, the distinguished FRB chairman, and the Bureau of the Budget expressed a distinct preference that the SEC assume the whole responsibility. Yet we still could not win over the Comptroller of the Currency. He continued to object publicly and by direct communication with members of Congress.[22] As a consequence, one liberal senator, Eugene McCarthy of Minnesota, attacked the SEC proposal in a speech, but by explaining our position, we averted any further objection on his part. Under the circumstances, we were asked to attend a meeting at the White House at which our differences would be resolved. They were, in effect, decided in our favor, and the administration formally supported the bill as amended. Subsequently, however, it was found that the Comptroller was continuing to object. He recommended that if the banking agencies did not have sufficient inherent existing

[18] See *Hearings before Subcommittee of Senate Committee on Banking and Currency on S. 1168*, 85th Cong., 1st Sess., May 20–24, 27, and 29, 1957, pp. 243–255.
[19] See *Senate Hearings* [SEC Legislation 1963], pp. 19, 54.
[20] See *Senate Hearings* [SEC Legislation 1963], p. 170.
[21] See *Senate Hearings* [SEC Legislation 1963], pp. 247–251.
[22] Saxon letter of Feb. 19, 1964, *House Hearings* [pt. 2, Investor Protection], p. 1357; also letter from William F. Kelly, President, American Bankers Assn., March 16, 1964, pp. 1367–1371; my letter of March 13, 1964, p. 1371.

powers, any statutory amendments should be made to the respective banking acts rather than to the Exchange Act. In fact, he denounced the president of the American Bankers Association in a letter circulated to the heads of all national banks, saying in effect that their spokesman had betrayed them.[23] The ABA asked whether I would hold a press conference, but we decided to reply in writing, so that there might be no misunderstanding. At this point we drafted a consciously intemperate letter to the chairman of the Interstate and Foreign Commerce Committee of the House stating our position with respect to disclosure of information by banks, the directive from the White House to the Comptroller to concur, and that this was irresponsible action on the part of any officer of the government. I was still reluctant to publish it, because that is not the way to run a government: settlement of differences with agencies without battles in the press should be a cardinal principle among government officials. As a consequence, I called a White House assistant and Kermit Gordon, the Director of the Bureau of the Budget, and read my letter to them. Since my letter was obviously belligerent, Mr. Gordon asked that I reframe it, which I was willing to do upon receiving his assurance that he too would write a letter, for publication, to Chairman Harris stating that the Comptroller was not speaking for the administration. His letter read in part as follows: [24]

It has come to our attention that in a letter to your committee, dated February 19, 1964, and in a statement of the same date, the Comptroller of the Currency expressed strong opposition to certain provisions of H.R. 6789 and S. 1642 which affect the Nation's banks. As you may have noted, neither the letter nor the testimony contained the usual advice from this Bureau as to relationship to the President's program. The views expressed, therefore, were the Comptroller's own views and they were in fact contrary to the administration position with respect to these provisions of the bill.

Despite this ultimatum we found that the Comptroller was still objecting and making every effort to kill the bill until the day it

[23] See *House Hearings* [pt. 2, Investor Protection], p. 1368–1371.
[24] *House Hearings* [pt. 2, Investor Protection], p. 1372.

was signed by the President. The question might be asked how a one-man regulatory agency could in this instance exercise such broad independence. This is particularly relevant since the Comptroller's office is technically part of an Executive Department, the Treasury. The answer seemed to lie in his own personal political support, goodwill generated by some of his progressive ideas in banking, plus the fact that the Comptroller of the Currency has a term appointment and can only be removed by the President "upon reasons to be communicated by him to the Senate." [25]

The other industry which began to raise questions was the insurance industry, but it was not yet fully mobilized. Only one man testified in the Senate. The principal objection raised was that reporting of information to the SEC would necessitate a different type of accounting (together with certified audits by outside public accounting firms) than had been used conventionally by the superintendents of insurance of all the states.[26] In order to avoid this obstacle, we entered into certain commitments by letter to Senator Robertson, assuring him that the accounting treatment had been and would remain for all practical purposes identical.[27] This did not satisfy the insurance industry, but objections were not vocal at the time, and their opposition was not yet effective.

As a consequence, the bill as it left the Senate committee generally remained intact with the exception that jurisdiction over banks was vested exclusively in the Federal banking regulatory authorities. I went to see various senators just prior to the meeting of the Senate Banking and Currency Committee, and particularly one Senator who had expressed opposition to the inclusion of the insurance industry in the bill. Since the committee was meeting at ten o'clock, I arranged to be in his office at eight-thirty that morning; but when I arrived, I found he had driven down with his former administrative assistant, who was then a leading counsel

---

[25] 12 U.S.C.A. ch. 1, 81.

[26] Testimony of Wm. C. Ridgeway, Jr., *Senate Hearings*, [SEC Legislation 1963], June 24, 1963, p. 228; see also letter and statement, p. 268.

[27] See my letter dated Aug. 30, 1963, *House Hearings* [pt. 1, Investor Protection], p. 85, at 88.

of the insurance industry. I said I might as well give up, but would like a moment of his attention. I was received courteously, although it was clear that I could not change the views which the Senator had reached. I never regretted having seen senators who opposed provisions of our bill, for thus they would learn directly why we took the opposite side, rather than learning about it secondhand, and they would also know that we were not ogres whom they might be willing to attack personally when they opposed our bill.

After passage through the committee, which voted down two amendments offered (including a proposed exemption for insurance company securities) the bill immediately went through the Senate without objection. The combined support of such members as Senator Robertson of Virginia and Senator Javits of New York, divergent both on party and regional lines, as well as in philosophy, undoubtedly had some influence.

We were now prepared for the presentation to the House. At this point, it may be worthwhile to note certain fundamental differences in dealing with the Senate and the House. One contrast is in the role of the chairman. In the Banking and Currency Committee of the Senate, for example, each member who had a view was listened to by the chairman and his position was given serious consideration regardless of which party he represented. This is especially true of that committee and its chairman, but it is inevitable by reason of the difference in the size of the two Houses and the consequently broader power that a single senator can wield. Yet in this comparison no generalization is entirely safe. Much depends on the particular chairman. One House chairman had lost all control over his committee. Congressman Harris, on the other hand, could not afford to be autocratic, but he wielded great authority. He was respected by his committee members of both parties. This point was verified by remarks of Congressman Broyhill, a Republican who praised the way in which Mr. Harris conducted his committee business.

Another difference in attitude stems from the role of the House over regulatory agencies, particularly with respect to the SEC, which Speaker Sam Rayburn regarded as one of his own progeny.

Recollection of the Speaker had not been lost, as evidenced by the remark of Chairman Harris: [28]

I don't believe you will find anybody today that has anything to do whatsoever with the securities business that would recommend the repeal of those acts of 1933 and 1934. . . . I am reminding you that when these acts were passed—I wasn't here, but Speaker Rayburn told me about it time after time—there was a great concern expressed and vigorous opposition, but it has stabilized. . . .

The House Interstate and Foreign Commerce Committee takes its oversight responsibility seriously. The accepted view is that it is not there simply to pass upon bills which an agency sponsors, but even more to insure that it is doing the job that Congress envisages, or not doing things to which it objects. Furthermore, its role as overseer extends beyond the Commission to the exchanges, as evidenced by the critical and uncomfortable questioning of the president of the New York Stock Exchange and also of the National Association of Securities Dealers (NASD) during one of the five hearings held in connection with the bill.[29]

A further difference that stood out as a result of this bill lay in the attitude of the Senate and the House toward getting it passed. The Senate assumed that a careful study had been made, which was true. It found that there was relatively little opposition and that a part of the bill had been considered, and acted upon, some years before in the Senate. As a consequence, they were ready for action and took it immediately. They even solicited our help in drafting the committee report, which may be almost as important as the bill itself. On the other hand, the House Interstate and Foreign Commerce Committee proceeded in exactly the other direction, on the basis of letting the bill rest for an extended period of time in order that any opposition to it could be allowed to develop. As one member described it, "you have to let the dust set-

---

[28] *House Hearings* [pt. 2, Investor Protection], p. 917.

[29] *House Hearings* [pt. 2, Investor Protection], concerning New York Stock Exchange, Feb. 4, 1963, pp. 1072–1150; concerning NASD [pt. 1, Investor Protection], Nov. 21, 1963, pp. 612–673.

tle" after its introduction in the House. Politically, this is a technique for ascertaining public reaction to the bill and is well adapted to any committee chairmen who have sensitive antennae.

### Obstacles in the House

After the Senate passed the bill in July of 1963,[30] the dust did indeed settle for a long time and the House subcommittee would not even consider scheduling the commencement of hearings. There was criticism. For example, the *New York Times* speculated why the committee should refuse to take up a good bill already passed by the Senate, but its view was of no avail.[31] What is a critical story in a New York paper to an Arkansas congressman? Chairman Harris made that point clear in a public hearing. One quickly recognizes the predominant power of a chairman in a House committee, where the House consists of 435 members, as compared with 100 senators. As to a hearing, we were basically at the chairman's mercy, although perhaps it could be that with his blessing the subcommittee chairman might go ahead and schedule a meeting on his own. In this case, the committee chairman so dominated the situation by reason of his knowledge and experience that no action was taken until he saw fit.

His attitude toward the Senate is quite revealing. In the first place he did not know it had passed our bill and in fact did not much care. Cooperation was practically nonexistent. I had gone to Chairman Harris and expressed the hope that he would not mind if our bill was first considered by the Senate. I wanted to avoid any notion that our obeisance to one chamber was greater than to the other. Jealousies develop, as demonstrated by the fate of the omnibus appropriations bill affecting our agency among others.

On October 21, the House subcommittee finally scheduled the commencement of hearings for November 19. We were given no

---

[30] S. 1642, 88th Cong. (July 1963): see Senator Robertson's Remarks in 110 CONG. REC. 17798 (Aug. 6, 1964).

[31] Editorial, "Why the Stalling, Mr. Harris?", N.Y. Times, Oct. 9, 1963; "Mystery Cloaks Market Hearings"; N.Y. Times, Nov. 17, 1963, § 3, p. 1, col. 1.

idea of their duration, and certainly no one at that time forecast that the hearings would, as they did, intermittently drag on with five installments until February 19, 1964. At the same time, in a letter from the subcommittee chairman, we were told that the hearings would not only cover the bill but any action we had taken under the Special Study of the Securities Markets, which had made numerous recommendations.[32] They not only reviewed the Special Study but included testimony from all the exchanges, and inquiries into the financial responsibility of broker-dealer firms and the performance of specialists on the New York Stock Exchange. In retrospect, these hearings proved beneficial both to the Commission and to the committee in the proper exercise of its oversight role. They placed a heavy responsibility on the agency to prepare itself to cover all aspects of the securities markets as well as the bill before Congress. Most of our best talent had to be mobilized for this purpose. Our first presentation to the House subcommittee extended from November 19 to 21, just preceding the death of the President. In general, the subjects that worried the committee primarily at this stage concerned banks and insurance companies and foreign securities.

There were five other questions, some of them representing a distinct attitude against further Federal intrusion into existing state supervision. One was whether the second (broker-dealer) part of our bill should make SEC supervision and registration applicable to persons engaged in the brokerage business exclusively in one state.[33] To some extent, this is almost an illusion today, for there is very little, if any, real securities business that is wholly intrastate in character. Yet there are some persons selling local oil royalties or certain types of securities in a local market. It was our opinion that all such fringe groups should fall under the same general regulatory pattern as the 95 percent of broker-dealers in the country (particularly since they were already subject to the antifraud provisions and our rules of financial responsibility). But this met with severe opposition from persons who emphasize

---

[32] See *House Hearings* [pt. 1, Investor Protection], Nov. 19, 1963, at pp. 43, 69.

[33] See *House Hearings* [pt. 2, Investor Protection], Dec. 3, 1963, at p. 733, at 735.

states' rights. Indeed, we always found ourselves challenged by the chairman when we insisted our proposal would not constitute a preemption of state regulation of securities. Since we could not satisfy his objections, we were doomed with respect to extending our jurisdiction over intrastate broker-dealers, but we did not regard this as basically serious. Another part of the bill involving states' rights concerned the insurance industry, which will be covered separately below.

Like encroachment upon states' rights, compulsory membership [34] in any trade association is also distasteful to many members of Congress. The proposal of our bill was to organize all broker-dealers to become members of an association—in all probability the National Association of Securities Dealers, the only one existing at the time (although they could form another)—and place upon that association the burden of supervision over its members. The objective here was to rely upon the principle of self-regulation already referred to (Chapter 2; Oversight and Self-regulation, p. 43). Although we did not say that self-regulation works perfectly in the securities industry, it takes many of the burdens off government, particularly in regulation of details, and vests it in an institution which can concentrate upon ethical practices beyond the reach of a statute. Particularly interesting in this connection was a reversal of roles: I found myself taking issue with the more conservative (Republican and certain Democratic) representatives, who expressed deep aversion to requiring membership in an organization which might in some ways be regarded as a trade association as well as a quasi-public agency organized pursuant to the authority of the Securities Exchange Act of 1934. Chairman Harris noted his prior objection to the proposal once made that all broadcasters become members of the National Association of Broadcasters. My view,[35] highly conservative, was that the United States government had no business becoming directly involved in supervision over a group of broker-dealers who were not yet members of any association, that they could become members of the National Association of Securities Dealers, or

[34] See *House Hearings* [pt. 1, Investor Protection], Nov. 19, 1963, at 101, 240, 249; Dec. 3, 1963, p. 743.
[35] See *House Hearings* [pt. 2, Investor Protection], Feb. 18, 1964, p. 1217.

form a new one, but that under any circumstances a minimum of government participation was advisable, so long as the job could be performed by a quasi-public association, which, in turn, was subject to the supervision of the SEC. It is surprising to find oneself in the dual role as a reformer and a mossback simultaneously. On this point Chairman Harris was amused to note that in the same corridor of the House of Representatives I was seen trying to convince a Republican congressman while a lawyer (chairman of the District of Columbia Republican Committee) was trying to persuade Congressman Long, a Louisiana Democrat, to the contrary. Once the hearings on a bill cease, the *ex parte* (lobbying) process intensifies.

Despite its attraction to persons who are generally opposed to government interference, our argument did not outweigh the principle that no one should be required to become a member of an association. I reached this conclusion after talking to every one of the thirty members on the House committee. It was impossible to dampen the opposition, generated at the outset, by a single large California firm, Insurance Securities, Inc., with 670 salesmen offering shares in one mutual fund.[36] There were three or four Western firms operating in the same manner through their own large sales forces, numbering in thousands. All these firms ultimately joined forces, but it can be fairly said that a single company, largely unaided, was able to alter a major provision of the bill. This group had long resisted becoming a member of the National Association of Securities Dealers, and in reality did not want any kind of regulation, pointing out they were selling only a single product or small group of products (mutual funds). They could enlist a number of different congressmen in their cause: those who did not believe in a closed shop, a few Populists who opposed Eastern domination, i.e., the NASD, and many others who felt that the NASD (composed of broker-dealers selling mutual funds) would be regulating their competitors (those who had their own sales forces). They further denounced it as an unconstitutional delegation of power. But they were faced with a dilemma which we emphasized to the House committee chairman:

---

[36] See *House Hearings* [pt. 2, Investor Protection], Jan. 21, 1964, at p. 836.

that if he favored raising the standards in the securities industry and refused to accept compulsory membership on the part of all persons in the industry in an association having that very objective, Congress must provide for some uniform regulation over those who were outside the regulatory pattern and give the SEC the very same authority over them that the NASD had over its members. This approach was not anticipated by the three or four groups engaged in selling mutual funds, though they had said earlier they did not object to regulation per se but objected only to compulsory membership in an association such as the NASD. On this point, Chairman Harris became adamant, and angry. Lobbyists can press too far, and hurt the cause. He recognized that they really did not want any kind of supervision despite their affirmation that they were willing to accept it, and he was responsible in large part for providing the Commission with new powers comparable to those of the NASD over its members.[37]

Another outburst occurred in the House committee on the market maker provision where, as earlier noted in the section on Negotiating the Bill, we had yielded to arguments made by industry. It stemmed from Congressman Dingell,[38] a liberal Democrat who generally supported the bill. Mr. Dingell and several other persons on the committee, though recognizing that we were embarked on a reform measure, nevertheless began to criticize us saying there was not a single provision in the bill which was objected to by the securities industry. The point had been made earlier, in the form of a question addressed by Congressman Staggers, the subcommittee chairman, to the chairman of the Industry Liaison Committee.[39] The inference was that we might become a tool of the industry, rather than independently express our views. Yet the political realities were such that if any major provision were not acceptable to the industry, there might have been such an outcry that even a hearing might not have been given to the bill in time. Specifically, those who claimed to support reform

---

[37] See Sec. 15(b)(8) of the Securities Exchange Act of 1934, as amended.
[38] See *House Hearings* [pt. 2, Investor Protection], Feb. 18, 1964, pp. 1221–1228.
[39] See *House Hearings* [pt. 1, Investor Protection], Nov. 21, 1963, p. 647.

bore down upon our compromise and suggested that persons making markets over the counter in securities of companies in which they were directors must be subject to the short-swing trading requirements. As already noted, we were accused of having made a "contract," a euphemistic word for sellout. The label is not flattering, but it is fundamental to keep faith with the industry and we needed its support. The net result was that the market maker provision was changed by the subcommittee against the industry and contrary to our recommendation, but the full committee restored the exemption. The decision was to leave this issue for discussion on the floor of the House when the bill finally came there. Since Mr. Dingell would be away, he asked Congressman Moss of California to offer his amendment (removing the exemption for the market maker). Mr. Moss being a very respected and effective Congressman who could fairly say this exemption unduly favored a special group within the securities industry, we felt that he might succeed and withdraw support of large segments of the industry and thus kill the bill. In order to avoid such a catastrophe at that point, I emphasized to him that his amendment might mobilize the opposition, that we had been working on this reform measure for over two years and did not think he ought to allow it to founder on such a narrow ground. On the day it went to the house he acceded.

In the meantime, another member of the House committee, Gillis Long, called me to say he was going to introduce another amendment that would affect the way broker-dealers do business on the over-the-counter market. He expressed his dissatisfaction with the NASD, and with Wall Street generally, and talked about some of the origins of the streak of Populism that characterized the Long family of Louisiana. With the aid of Chairman Harris we headed this off with the promise that hearings on his amendment would be held at a later date. Congressman Long was defeated in the primary shortly afterward.

At this point it may be worthwhile to note the role of the White House. In general, a bill of this type gets relatively little help from the White House. As noted earlier, the Bureau of the Budget acting as an arm of the White House had gone so far as to say that the bill was "in accord with the program of the President." [40] This is a relatively high designation, but I was subsequently told by one of the Senate chiefs of staff that no one cared very much what the Bureau of the Budget said so long as it did not disapprove the bill. Of course, if the President included it in a White House message, it would then be taken seriously as a part of the administration program. Happily, we had discussed the bill several times with counsel in the White House, so that he was fully aware of its existence and we had also brought it to the attention of Mrs. Esther Petersen, who represented the consumer there. Perhaps because of these several influences, and because the bill was through the Senate and out of committee in the House, and had reasonably good prospects for passage, it was mentioned in the President's consumer message and on June 23 was included as one of thirty bills that the President wanted to see passed before the end of that session of Congress. [41] This affirmation was of considerable help in establishing priority in the minds of the leadership in the House. On the other hand, White House support was not so strong as to give the bill a partisan flavor.

As noted in the section on Reception in the Senate, there was a constant motif of opposition from Mr. Saxon when our bill was in the Senate and the House, and even up to the date of its signing by the President. Yet it can be said that, while politically effective almost to the point of killing our bill, his opposition had been blunted, and its logic undermined, by the amendment we sponsored that in administering the disclosure and registration requirements applicable to bank securities, all powers were to vest automatically in the appropriate Federal banking regulatory authorities rather than the SEC. To remove any vestige of doubt, the House committee added a provision: "none of the rules, . . . issued or adopted by the Commission . . . shall be in any way binding . . . upon any such banks." [42] Thus no one could say that we were grasping for power or "empire building."

As already indicated, unless the principle of registration and

[40] *House Hearings* [pt. 1, Investor Protection], p. 64.
[41] N.Y. Times, June 24, 1964, p. 12, col. 6.
[42] Section 12(i) of the Securities Exchange Act of 1934, as amended.

supervision of bank stocks was preserved, it is obvious that effective opposition could be mobilized by the stock insurance companies on the ground of uniformity of treatment. They were second only to bank stocks in their importance among public concerns whose securities were traded over the counter.[43] One of the greatest obstacles in having a successful bill passed affecting insurance stocks was the traditional attitude of the industry to avoid Federal regulation at all cost. Thus far the industry has been highly successful. Our bill did not in fact relate to the great mutual insurance companies at all, but simply to stock insurance companies. Our thesis was that investors should have adequate protection and information about the companies in which they were security holders, whether industrial or otherwise.

To demonstrate the need for these protections, in our Special Study of the Securities Markets we had marshaled data which clearly demonstrated that the information available to the public investor as to insurance companies was grievously wanting, in fact more than in any other industry.[44] The reports and proxies these companies were sending out were minimal and uninformative.[45] Present reporting was geared to the protection of policy-holders, not to inform the security owners. Furthermore, there were numerous examples of abuses and fraud in the promotion of stock insurance companies, which had burgeoned since World War II.[46]

By the time of the House hearings, the insurance industry had begun to mobilize its forces. Indeed, Chairman Harris in the first set of hearings had spoken out and said that if they wanted to be heard this was their last chance and they must do so. He sought to test the intensity of their opposition.

To generate political resistance, the companies could most effectively operate through the insurance commissioners, who share with the industry itself a desire to maintain exclusive state supervision. These gentlemen came in groups to Washington to call on the chairman and other members of the House. Not least

[43] *House Hearings* [pt. 1, Investor Protection], Nov. 19, 1963, p. 119.

[44] *Special Study*, pt. 3, p. 40 (1963).

[45] *Ibid.*

[46] *House Hearings* [pt. 1, Investor Protection], Nov. 19, 1963, pp. 199–205.

conspicuous among them, of course, was the Commissioner of Insurance of Arkansas, the state of the committee chairman. Being a man of political acumen, Chairman Harris was keenly aware of what was going on, but he also recognized they represented a powerful political force, coming from every state and exerting influence on every representative. Commenting at a hearing upon a statement by an insurance commissioner, he said, "It seems to me that there should be a meeting of the minds somewhere between those of you who are supposed to be regulated and those who are supposed to be regulating." [47] At one point in his office he indicated his appreciation of their attitude, when the insurance commissioners said, "We do not want SEC registration." He immediately said, "I want to get this straight: When you say, 'we,' are you speaking for yourselves or are you fronting for the insurance industry?" This direct confrontation does not signify that the chairman was impervious to the political power of the commissioners and the industry.

A number of the leading people in the insurance industry have confidentially advised that a few of the state insurance commissioners are captives of the insurance companies (New York being a notable exception). I was particularly interested in noting that in our meeting with the commissioners, one of the principal spokesmen was a highly articulate representative, a deputy superintendent from a Western state. Finding that he was subsequently replaced and inquiring why, I learned that a financial scandal had been publicized and he had quickly resigned. Thereupon the insurance superintendents had been wise enough to appoint as their head the Commissioner of Insurance of the state of California, who attempted to salvage the situation on their behalf. Perhaps more than anyone in the industry, he made a vigorous presentation.[48] He argued that if the banks were to be permitted to be regulated by several Federal agencies, why could not the insurance industry remain regulated by their proper (state) regulatory agency. There were several answers. For example, there was a high degree of disuniformity in administration

---

[47] See generally *House Hearings* [pt. 1, Investor Protection], Jan. 22, 1964, pp. 889–923.
[48] Statement of Stafford R. Grady, *House Hearings* [pt. 2, Investor Protection], Jan. 22, 1964, p. 868.

among the fifty states, with some commissioners who were not willing or equipped to take action and others like New York who were vigorous. Second, the role of the commissioners of insurance was to protect the policyholder, not the shareholder, and this would add a totally new function and responsibility. Finally, we made probably the strongest presentation in the course of the hearing demonstrating the need to include insurance companies and cataloguing misstatements made about the industry.[49] At the same time, Chairman Harris was obviously affected, as were his fellow committee members who represented states having many insurance companies, such as Massachusetts. The argument for the tradition against Federal regulation of insurance was strong[50] and Congress was in search of compromise, which we had been unwilling to make lest this be the basis upon which jurisdiction over both banks and insurance companies could be stricken from the bill. It became apparent that a compromise was a political necessity. The following colloquy summarizes the reaction of Chairman Harris:[51]

MR. HARRIS. Of course I will say to Mr. Cary when we go into this one big issue of the insurance people, very frankly I think you have made a very good case. On the other hand, I think they have come up with some improvements [in] which they propose, notwithstanding what you say in your report here. It appears to me that they are supposed to do precisely the same thing that you say that needs to be done and that it has become a question of who is going to do it. It is unfortunate that we had to get in between the vise here, and I hope you understand what kind of vise I am talking about.

MR. CARY. Yes, sir; I understand.

MR. HARRIS. We do not like to be put in that position but it does seem to me that there might be some merit in their program if they propose to carry out the requirements that you have indicated if there are proper reports made.

MR. CARY. Mr. Chairman, I can only hope the rational provision prevails. . . .

---

[49] *House Hearings* [pt. 2, Investor Protection], Feb. 18, 1964, pp. 1203–1216.
[50] *House Hearings* [pt. 2, Investor Protection], Jan. 22, 1964, p. 890.
[51] *House Hearings* [pt. 2, Investor Protection], Feb. 19, 1964, p. 1293.

We wanted to salvage the principle of disclosure and the application of proxy and insider trading rules, but how much erosion could we avoid? The bill was redrafted and presented to the committee to provide an exemption for insurance companies if all of the following conditions were met. [Section 12(g)(2)(G)]: [52]

(i) Such insurance company is required to and does file an annual statement with the Commissioner of Insurance . . . and such annual statement [substantially] conforms to that prescribed by the National Association of Insurance Commissioners . . . [N.A.I.C.].

(ii) Such insurance company is subject to regulation by its domiciliary State of proxies, consents, or authorizations . . . and such regulation conforms to that prescribed by the [N.A.I.C.].

(iii) After July 1, 1966, the purchase and sales of securities issued by such insurance company by beneficial owners, directors, or officers of such company are subject to regulation (including reporting) by its domiciliary State substantially in the manner provided in section 16 of this title. . . .

Though not to our liking, number (iii) offers an interesting way for the Federal government to impose uniformity of laws among the states.

In retrospect, I am not sure that the insurance industry gained much in victory. Several of the leaders in the industry in New England agreed that it was most unfortunate that their spokesmen were the marginal companies that did not want to have this information become available. They were centered in the West, South, and Southwest where stock insurance companies were most actively promoted.[53] This bill would not have affected the large mutuals at all and indeed would seldom affect the great stock companies which had already assumed responsibility to their shareholders. The only ones that it would strike hard were the small concerns recently promoted which were reluctant to provide the information, to furnish adequate proxies, and to accept the laws against insider trading. Furthermore, the bill as it stood

---

[52] Section 12(g)(2)(G) of the Securities Exchange Act of 1934, as amended (in 1964).

[53] See *House Hearings* [pt. 1, Investor Protection], Nov. 19, 1963, p. 120, and Appendix C, p. 199.

already required that a company which goes to the public for funds must register the stock issue with the SEC.[54] Some insurance executives regard this compromise as an unfortunate development and wish in fact that the provision had been retained making their companies subject to the jurisdiction of the SEC. But a long tradition against Federal regulation ultimately prevailed. The big companies find political alliance with the small ones at times beneficial. They have been unwilling to take the leadership in improving the status of the young or promotional stock insurance companies in the way that the large firms in the securities industry have forced higher standards upon the smaller ones.

One final obstacle in getting legislation through was in connection with foreign securities. Here again, as with the market maker provision, several liberal members of the House committee concluded that the SEC would fail to meet its obligations if the bill provided in effect that foreign securities should be exempted initially.[*] The Commission's view was that it is extremely difficult to enforce disclosure and proxy requirements with respect to securities of foreign companies which have not sold stock in the American market, but whose securities have been purchased by Americans and are now traded in this market.[55] In fact, there is involved an important issue of the extraterritorial application of American law to foreign corporations. The House, however, was adamant on this point, perhaps because of the views of a principal staff adviser and its unfriendly attitude toward foreign securities generally, and therefore provided that all foreign securities should be subject to the act with power in the Commission to exempt them under specified circumstances.[56] This created a new lobby opposing the bill in the last days of the session of the House. We recognized that any group of congressmen objecting to the bill might persuade the chairman that it was controversial

---

[*] It remained applicable unless the Commission should find the existence of a substantial public market and that continued exemption is not in the public interest or consistent with the protection of investors.

[54] Pursuant to the Securities Act of 1933, § 5.

[55] *House Hearings* [pt. 2, Investor Protection], Feb. 19, 1964, p. 1284 et ff.

[56] Section 12(g)(3) of the Securities Exchange Act of 1934 as amended.

and not worth fighting for. The fear aroused was that all trading would be illegal in the securities of foreign companies that had not complied. We took the position that it did not matter which way the bill was written, because it gave the Securities and Exchange Commission considerable latitude. However, these assurances did not satisfy the foreign securities dealers, particularly after the tax equalization bill, and they expressed the fear that this would dry up the foreign securities markets. As a consequence they were lobbying with the Treasury and the State Department and congressmen, and even among members of the Senate in the hope that if the bill should pass the House there would have to be a conference between the Senate and the House, and the Senate version (our own original version) would prevail, or the bill would die at the end of the session. They had already obtained a letter from Senator Williams (New Jersey), the subcommittee chairman, saying he thought there would have to be a conference on the foreign securities issue. The *New York Times*, perhaps the staunchest supporter of our bill, had editorially attacked the House version.[57] No matter how small, a lobby can induce Congress to shy away from a bill which no member is strongly pushing.

In an effort to soften the potentially harsher position of the House bill, we indicated to the Senate that in the administration of the foreign securities provision the House version (if adopted) would still leave us with the power to exempt foreign securities for at least a year before the issue of their inclusion was taken up. This commitment was written [58] into a letter to Senator Robertson and Chairman Harris, and though it did not satisfy the foreign securities interests, nevertheless none of the senators insisted upon a conference. In my concern over this flurry I told the president of the NASD, which was officially favoring the bill, that he and the foreign securities dealers in his organization might have to bear responsibility for killing it, and asked him if that was his wish. To prove otherwise, he went with me to the offices of several senators and again pledged his support in favor of the bill as

[57] Editorial, "Action on Investor Safeguards," N.Y. Times, July 4, 1964.
[58] See my letter to Sen. Robertson dated Aug. 5, 1964, CONG. REC. 18128 (Aug. 5, 1964).

it stood. When the House bill was submitted to the Senate and voted upon, the only step taken was that Senator Javits on the floor of the Senate asked in a colloquy with Senator Robertson whether the Committee would maintain careful scrutiny of how the foreign securities provision was being administered, and Senator Robertson assured him that this would be done.[59]

Despite all of the objections that had been raised to a "noncontroversial bill," it might be expected that by the time the bill had passed the full committee of the House (30 members) and had already been through the Senate once, there would be little likelihood of its being killed on the House floor. However, the deadline was approaching: the second session was drawing to a close and the Republican convention was already near when the House committee was to vote upon it. Further, we were much concerned whether any action would be taken upon it by the Senate once the debate on the civil rights bill was under way. There remained the last hurdle in the House—the Rules Committee presided over by "Judge" Howard W. Smith of Virginia. When I went to Chairman Harris to inquire when the House would take up the bill, he indicated almost in consternation that he could not get a rule from Judge Smith. The latter was chairman of the board of the Alexandria (Va.) National Bank and had received a call from a friend in a national bank in Richmond who had raised some objection. It was not clear in his mind as to how the bill affected banks, but it was controversial. Furthermore, Judge Smith indicated that he had talked twice to Mr. Saxon, Comptroller of the Currency, who was still lobbying against it. As a consequence, he was not in a mood to fix a time for the bill's presentation on the House floor and Chairman Harris was deeply disturbed. Mr. Harris had serious opposition in the primary for the first time in his career and had to go back to his constituency, which meant that he could not be around. Even Congressman Carl Albert, majority floor leader, told me that there was no action he could take. As a consequence, I asked Chairman Harris whether there was anything we could do and suggested two things which he accepted, one that at my request Senator Robertson of Virginia would telephone Judge Smith of his state and express his interest in the bill, and second,

---

[59] 110 Cong. Rec. 18384 (1964).

119

that the American Bankers Association might talk with the Judge. Both these steps were carried out effectively and the result was that a week later Judge Smith said that he would issue a rule and the bill could go before the House.

The bill was actually taken up after the Republican convention and by that time we thought it would go through without difficulty. However, Congressman Farbstein of New York, having just examined the bill, raised questions which neither the chairman nor other spokesmen could clarify on the floor and threw it into the air again.[60] Luckily, after Mr. Farbstein's questions were asked, the House was adjourned for the day. Chairman Harris was by no means confident, saying that no one can tell what the House will do with a bill like this if questions are raised on the floor. So Commissioner Cohen (my successor) and I went over to see Congressman Farbstein and clarified all the problems he had raised. He said he would be satisfied if we wrote a letter of explanation, which we produced for him before the House met the next morning, and he offered no further objection.[61] The bill then swiftly passed the House. The designation of the bill offers an interesting illustration of House procedure. After it was passed as H.R. 6793, Chairman Harris asked the House to take the Senate bill (S. 1642), strike all material after the enacting clause and insert the provisions of H.R. 6793, then send S. 1642 as so amended to the Senate, and lay H.R. 6793 on the table.[62] Under Senate procedure, had H.R. 6793 gone over to the Senate, it would have been treated as a new bill and referred to a committee, absent unanimous consent to passage. Furthermore, the Senate might have bridled over the fact that its own bill was not acted upon. This procedure thus allowed House legislative history to be made under the H.R. 6793 designation, while still observing the proper protocol with the Senate.

Two comments in retrospect may be worth making: in the first place, it becomes clear that opposition of any magnitude may kill a bill which is without strong sponsorship. True, the exchanges were for it but not beyond testifying on its behalf. They did not

[60] 110 CONG. REC. 17919 (1964).
[61] 110 CONG. REC. 18181 (1964).
[62] 110 CONG. REC. 18193 (1964).

120

exert their influence at the "grass roots"—among the members of Congress, until the very last days. Mr. Saxon by talking with Judge Smith and a Richmond banker almost kept the bill in the Rules Committee ("bottled up" in the words of the critics). An objection from Congressman Moss as to the market maker exemption—a claim that it was a "contract," or a giveaway to industry—might have generated enough opposition from the liberals to amend the bill and force a conference when time was running low. The foreign securities holders might have prevailed on a New York congressman to offer an amendment which would have raised a question. If representatives of the insurance industry had been more alert, they might have mobilized some congressmen to oppose it on the floor of the House. Even Congressman Farbstein's question (seeking information and not intended as an obstacle) could have created confusion among some of the members on the House floor. At this point, Congressman Harris was talking about watering down the bill further, and in effect ready to give up much of what we had fought for. Though his authority over our bill was autocratic vis-à-vis the Commission, and his effectiveness with his committee demonstrated, he felt powerless to head off opposition on the House floor.

Second, to demonstrate how little some congressmen know about the implications of legislation they are dealing with, a company manufacturing gravestones in New England got in touch with one of the members of the Interstate and Foreign Commerce Committee and said it was the only company in the industry to be covered by the bill. It further claimed it would be forced to make disclosures to all its competitors and hence the bill was unfair. This was only a few days before the bill went before the House. The congressman asked the staff assistant whether the provisions would apply to the company and was surprised to find that they would; it was a sizable publicly held concern. He then asked if there was anything he could do about it, including amending the bill at this late date, and was told it was probably too late. Though he sponsored the bill nominally and spoke on its behalf from a statement prepared by the staff, he accepted the disclosure provision reluctantly and was assured that if the gravestone company had any special contracts it could ask for confidential treatment.[63] This incident clearly demonstrates how little legislators may know about the details of a bill which they are of record as favoring. Chairman Harris and other congressmen, on the other hand, worked tirelessly with our staff to understand the technical aspects of the bill, without any expectation of personal or political benefit from their efforts.

We clarified these few points which were worrying the Senate committee, and a day later the House version passed the Senate without a conference. Our bill was one of several which were considered while the civil rights debate was going on in the Senate. Fortunately, it went through before the end of the session and was signed by the President two weeks later, on August 20, 1964. If it had not passed then, the process would have had to be undertaken all over again.

---

[63] 110 CONG. REC. 18181 (1964).

# 5 | Generalizations

## and Conclusions

### Introduction

There has been a vast body of literature criticizing the independent regulatory commissions and their procedures, but little discussing how they can do better the job for which they were established. Perhaps this is due to the predominance of writings by lawyers whose emphasis focuses more upon fairness than upon substance. Certainly there is no formula uniformly applicable to them: since they are not fungible, each commission would have to be considered separately. The attempt has been to show, impressionistically, how politics affects the way the agencies carry on and to inquire whether and how some vitality can be preserved.

First of all, as in the Introduction, let us once again place the commissions in context. There is probably as much adjudication and rule making affecting private interests in the Departments headed by Cabinet officers as in these independent agencies. Examples include the Immigration and Naturalization Service (of Justice), the Board of Contract Appeals (of Defense), the Commodity Exchange Authority (of Agriculture), and the Food and

Drug Administration and Social Security Administration (of Health, Education, and Welfare). There has been relatively little study comparing the caliber of adjudication and rule making in the regular Departments with that in the commissions we have been considering. Somehow regulatory activity in the Departments has received slight attention from bar associations, law teachers, and law reviews, while the independent agencies have been subject to almost microscopic examination. Yet it is all administrative law. Perhaps the subject matter is responsible: the independent agencies, as already noted, touch upon fields where major business interests are involved. Compare, for example, a single decision involving the television industry with a spate of decisions involving individual immigration permits. Where might we expect to find the pressures, well-known counsel, and strong industry representation?

Further, by comparison, these agencies seem to be constantly subjected to political criticism, more than many government organizations which affect the economy to a greater degree. Whether we think of a housing or an antipoverty program, or an action taken by the Department of Agriculture, Interior, or Defense, a decision may affect the future not only of companies, but of whole communities, without receiving the same volume of public comment. To illustrate, one need only turn to the Bureau of Reclamation in the Department of the Interior, which is one of five bureaus under the Assistant Secretary for Water and Power Development. This Bureau, concerned with power and water projects in the Western states, awarded contracts in fiscal year 1963 amounting to more than 175 million dollars, almost triple the total amount spent by all the independent regulatory agencies in that year.[1] Thus again, the difference probably seems to lie in the fact that independent agencies affect private industry more directly on a day-to-day basis.

The silent premise seems to be that somehow independent agencies ought always to be alert and effective (not like government as a whole). At one time in the thirties they were treated as the salvation to many government problems, the preserver of our

[1] 1963 SEC'Y INT. ANN. REP. 170.

124

economic liberties. The very structure of an independent agency was thought to provide an independence and an expertise, "a judgelike wisdom, balance, and insight," that could not otherwise be achieved. After the euphoria of the New Deal and following World War II, they lost caste and were referred to disparagingly and with suspicion as the fourth branch of the government. Somehow the public and writers seemed to expect too much of regulatory agencies, with the hope for their achievements gyrating from unbounded optimism to despondency. Perhaps our objective should be to prevent illusions from being created rather than to foster them and then suffer them to be shattered.

Despite their important regulation of commerce, the independent agencies have a relatively limited role. Even the President seems scarcely to appreciate this fact. In a moment of crisis involving an industry he will probably expect too much of the agency. For example, can the Federal Power Commission do more than offer legislative proposals to meet a power failure such as we had in the Northeast in the winter of 1965? President Johnson immediately telephoned Chairman Swidler, but was there anything that the FPC could actually do at that moment? Or can the SEC identify a market decline and take measures soon enough to check it? [2] Does it share a seat with the Federal Reserve Board and the Treasury, whose economic power is much broader though by no means omnipotent? Its present role and capabilities are limited: to maintain fair and honest securities markets, and to keep the public investor informed. Yet in the event of a market break, the President, groping for a "solution" and believing strongly in action, may be raising these same inquiries.

### The Hector-Minow Proposal

As their valedictory statements, two leading members of Federal regulatory bodies, Louis J. Hector of the CAB and Newton N. Minow of the FCC, independently recommended a transfer of

---

[2] See Robbins, The Securities Markets: Operations and Issues (1966), ch. 5 (Criteria in the Securities Market).

the judicial functions of their agencies to an administrative court.[3] In consequence, the impression may be abroad that their recommendations represent the judgment and experience of responsible commissioners by the time of their departure. On the basis of my three and a half years at the SEC, I should like to record a vigorous dissent. Of course, I speak with competence only as to one agency, but I am happy to find these views are endorsed by thoughtful members of several others.[4]

Before indicating my strong differences, I should like to note the basic theses of Mr. Hector and Mr. Minow:

First, they charge that the multimember "independent" commissions have failed to discharge their basic responsibility for developing broad policies and standards governing the industries they regulate. Because the members of the commissions have been unable to reconcile basic differences among themselves and have been preoccupied with relatively minor details, policy making has been relegated to decisions in particular cases. The result, it is alleged, has been confusion among both the regulators and the regulated.

Second, they say the administrative agencies have performed their adjudicatory function poorly and unfairly because their members (1) must act as both prosecutors and judges and (2) are unable to devote the time needed to become familiar with the records or to think through the policy issues involved in the cases they must decide.

Third, they claim that the "independence" of the administrative agencies has hindered the coordination of policy between the various government agencies having overlapping regulatory jurisdiction over particular areas of the economy.

Mr. Hector and Mr. Minow, therefore, have concluded that adjudicatory, legislative, and prosecution responsibilities are incompatible functions and should not be combined in a single agency.

[3] Letter from Newton N. Minow to the President, May 31, 1963 (available from the Federal Communications Commission); Hector, *Problems of the C.A.B. and the Independent Regulatory Commissions,* 69 YALE L. J. 931 (1960). But see Kintner, *The Current Ordeal of the Administrative Process: In Reply to Mr. Hector,* 69 YALE L.J. 965 (1960).

[4] See, for example, Elman, *A Note on Administrative Adjudication,* 74 YALE L.J. 652, 655 (1965).

They have recommended that the adjudicatory functions of administrative agencies be transferred to separate administrative courts and that development of policy through rule making be concentrated in a single executive appointed by and responsible to the President.

I fully agree with many of their objectives. As Judge Henry J. Friendly[5] has effectively demonstrated in his critique of the administrative process, the development of regulatory standards is a primary responsibility of the administrative agencies. I do, however, take issue that the cause of any failure to make policy lies in the commingling of functions and that divorce of the judicial role is the appropriate remedy. I freely confess that most of my views have already been expressed by Professors Carl A. Auerbach of Minnesota,[6] Kenneth Culp Davis of Chicago,[7] Walter Gellhorn of Columbia[8] and Judge Friendly.[9] The only increment, therefore, is that my recent experience confirms their conclusions.

The questions we are concerned with here involve the means by which the regulatory agency should carry out its job. As already noted in the Introduction, rule making and adjudication are two of the regulatory methods used by the agencies. Generally speaking, when its action affects the interests of a group, the agency takes the legislative route: rule making; when it affects the interests of identifiable individuals or business entities, the quasi-judicial route: adjudication. At least as to the SEC, each approach is a necessary element of the regulatory process; to divorce them would make regulation incomplete and ineffective.

I start from the basic premise, a premise of good management whether in business or government, that authority and responsibility should be centralized in the same hands. If not, differences of opinion may develop and the policy directives set by the administrator may be frustrated by the court. This is a live possibil-

[5] FRIENDLY, op. cit.
[6] Auerbach, Some Thoughts on the Hector Memorandum, 1960 WIS. L. REV. 183; Should Administrative Agencies Perform Adjudicatory Functions? 1959 WIS. L. REV. 95.
[7] 1 DAVIS, ADMINISTRATIVE LAW § 1.04 (Supp. 1965).
[8] GELLHORN & BYSE, ADMINISTRATIVE LAW 1018–1024 (4th ed. 1960).
[9] In addition to his book, see Friendly, A Look at the Federal Administrative Agencies, 60 COLUM. L. REV. 429, 441 (1960).

ity. In fact, transfer of the SEC's adjudicatory functions would fragment the responsibility for the development of policy and standards in the securities markets and thus increase the certainties which Mr. Hector and Mr. Minow have sought to avoid.

Further, in my opinion, the interaction of informal administrative decisions, formal cases, and rule making is both fruitful and necessary. The vast bulk of SEC work, referred to in Chapter 3, consists of processing registration statements, periodic reports, proxy solicitation material, applications for exemptions, and requests for advisory letters under the various acts it administers. These activities are administrative in nature; they do not fit the dichotomy of rule making and adjudication. As financial lawyers know so well, most of this is handled informally by conference. It enriches our experience perhaps as much as litigated cases. Without concrete examples, policy formulation might become more sterile and unrealistic. It is not easy to make policy in a vacuum. In the words of Mark S. Massel of the Brookings Institution: "Policy formulation is a never-ending process. It calls for feed-back of ideas and information coming from the administration of existing policies. New problems arise that cannot be foreseen when rules are developed. As conditions change, they may require changes in policy." [10]

Mr. Hector and Mr. Minow advance two propositions warranting a specific reply: (1) that an independent regulatory commission having combined functions may be incapable of policy determination, and (2) that without the divorce of the judicial function, adjudication cannot be fair and of acceptable quality.

*Policy Determination.* As to the first I would question their conclusion that transfer of the judicial function is a prerequisite for a commission to concentrate on policy. "Policy" is not easily defined and Messrs. Hector and Minow have been vague in defining it. In the case of the SEC, it can be articulated in diverse ways: adopting rules, issuing statements of policy, assigning priorities in areas of enforcement, or choosing between alternatives in litigated cases. Indeed, the decision whether to take no action, to resolve a matter informally, or to resort to administrative pro-

[10] Massel, *The Regulatory Process*, 26 LAW & CONTEMP. PROB. 181, 186 (1961).

ceedings is often a crucial question of policy. As both Messrs. Hector and Minow recognize, there is no sharp line between the judicial role and policy making.

The judicial function, whether performed by judges or members of administrative agencies, is not limited to the mechanical task of applying established principles to the facts of record. A great many judicial decisions, to some extent, reflect policy considerations. A good illustration of the difficulty in drawing a line appears in Mr. Hector's own paper where he concludes that the selection of an airline route is policy and of the particular airline to operate over it is judicial,[11] even though (as Professor Auerbach has pointed out) [12] the choice of the airline may affect the characteristics of the route.

During my experience at the SEC the members of the commission were able to concentrate on policy questions. A substantial segment (almost half) of our time over three years was devoted to basic questions, through focusing on the Special Study of the Securities Markets and the mutual fund industry, on legislative recommendations, and on important rule making or adjudicatory matters. Concentration on policy is largely a problem of management. In order to carry out any broad-scale studies and devote a substantial fraction of commission time to them, the agency must be willing to delegate authority to its staff for the handling of the bulk of routine matters (see Chap. 3, page 85). At the same time, I must acknowledge the frustration of working with a large commission (as in some of the agencies) in arriving at a consensus on any policy issue.

As to agency procedures, Mr. Hector's description of the CAB's method in routing and rate cases effectively demonstrates that reliance on traditional judicial fact-finding techniques in the making of broad policy decisions by administrative agencies can be overdone. These decisions must rest on an expert analysis of complex economic data. The techniques of direct and cross-examination, the application of technical rules of evidence and the use of hearing examiners as the primary deciders unduly circumscribe and delay the policy making process. Mr. Hector's own examples

[11] HECTOR, *op. cit.*, note 3, at 934.
[12] AUERBACH, *op. cit.*, note 6, 196.

of the CAB's procedures provide an argument not for separation of functions but against the overjudicialization of the administrative process. The job of economic regulation was delegated to administrative agencies rather than the courts primarily to avoid the use of judicial methods. Administrative agencies can and should be flexible in the techniques utilized in the performance of their functions. Frankly, I am concerned that we are all concentrating upon judicialization at the expense of the merits, i.e., what the agency is there to do.

Mr. Hector suggests a procedure for developing policy that parallels the approach the SEC took in its Special Study. He says that a well-run agency would handle a problem of policy by blocking out a few basic decisions at the top level and then designating staff to do the necessary research, to process and systematize the data, and to develop an overall program. In making the Special Study a variety of techniques were used: (1) industry questionnaires to accumulate and systematize basic quantitative data; (2) historical, economic, and legal research to evaluate the data accumulated and the alternative solutions suggested; (3) investigative techniques to explore in depth certain problems; (4) public hearings to highlight specific trouble spots within the securities industry; (5) industry conferences to subject the basic data and research to the test of business experience. But perhaps most important was a continuing discussion among the staff of the Special Study, the Commission and its regular staff, and persons from the securities industry, the legal profession, and the universities.

Such a task could not have been accomplished within the relatively short time allowed if the study had been compelled to operate within the rigid framework of the traditional judicial process.

While reevaluation on the scale of the Special Market Study can serve an invaluable function in providing new vigor to a regulatory program, policy making must be a continuing process. A commission should have staff members on a permanent basis who are removed from the treadmill of routine business and who can devote their time to the formulation of long-range programs. This precludes the parsimonious budgets under which many of the regulatory agencies operated during the postwar period. As indicated in Chapter 2, deep cuts in the SEC budget had been made in the early 1950s at just the time when the securities markets began to expand rapidly.

Another point already noted (in Chapter 3) but not adequately appreciated is that "policy" can sometimes best be made through adjudication. Basic to the Hector-Minow position is a dislike of such policy making. But even though formulation of policy by rule making has many advantages over *ad hoc* determinations in particular cases, sometimes policy should be made in the context of particular cases. The relegation of policy making to the adjudicatory process is not necessarily, as Mr. Hector and Mr. Minow suggest, the result of the inability of agency members to reconcile their differences and to free themselves of preoccupation with minor details. In many situations, an agency's experience with a particular problem is too limited to allow for meaningful rule making. Complex policy decisions, moreover, can sometimes best be formulated by focusing on one aspect of a broad problem at a particular time. A rule oftentimes cannot be refined sufficiently to achieve its purpose without affecting other anticipated business activities.

An administrator under the Hector-Minow proposals would be shorn of this policy making tool. He would not be able to utilize the adjudicatory process as effectively as has the SEC, for example, in enunciating a clear policy against trading on the basis of inside information [13] or in fashioning an effective weapon against fraudulent "boiler room" operations.[14] At most, the administrator could only hope to persuade an administrative court that on the basis of experience which the court had not shared, achievement of these regulatory goals could best be accomplished through the adjudicatory process rather than through rule making.

---

[13] *See* In the Matter of *Cady, Roberts & Co.*, 40 SEC. 907 (1961), discussed in Chap. 3, p. 82.

[14] See *MacRobbins & Company*, Securities Exchange Act Release No. 6846 (July 11, 1962), affirmed, *sub. nom. Berko v. Securities and Exchange Commission*, 316 F. 2d 137 (2d Cir. 1963), discussed in Cohen & Rabin, *Broker-Dealer Selling Practice Standards: The Importance of Administrative Adjudication in Their Development*, 29 LAW & CONTEMP. PROB. 691 (1964).

Finally, Mr. Hector has taken the position that the plans and policies of the Civil Aeronautics Board are not coordinated in any way with those of other government agencies. I have no panacea for meeting the broad problems of the transportation industry— the competition between railroads, buses, trucks, barge lines, and the airlines—but I submit this problem of coordination is not one which a separate administrator rather than separate commissions will resolve. It is certainly true that an overall Department of Transportation (at Cabinet level) is needed, but that is not what Mr. Hector advocated.

By way of analogy, one might point to the banking industry, which at the Federal level is governed by the seven-man Federal Reserve Board, the three-man Federal Deposit Insurance Corporation, and the one-man Comptroller of the Currency. It is having problems almost comparable to those of the transportation industry. I doubt whether conflicting views would be resolved to the satisfaction of all by the appointment of a single policy administrator for each of these three regulatory agencies. Whether *all three* should be combined is again a separate problem that is not before us.

*Fairness and Quality in Adjudication.*[15] "But is the cost too great?" ask Messrs. Hector and Minow, that is, in terms of time allotted to administrative and legislative functions at the expense of fairness and quality in adjudication. I believe not. I suspect that the elimination of the adjudicatory functions from an administrative body might result in lower standards of quality, for an administrative court exercising only adjudicatory responsibilities would not have the overall regulatory experience necessary to meet the policy questions before it. Furthermore, a narrower job will attract lesser men, and it is hard enough now to recruit persons of ability and experience as commissioners. If there is overjudicialization, quality suffers, since the commission does not have the benefit of the combined judgment and experience of the staff on problems which are essentially policy positions. I am convinced that there should be much greater delegation of minor ad-

---

[15] This point is more fully developed in Cary, *Why I Oppose the Divorce of the Judicial Function from Federal Regulatory Agencies,* 51 A.B.A.J. 33, at 37 (1965).

ministrative matters, as well as initial decision making. Mr. Hector attempts to draw a line between policy and adjudication; a better one might be between the important and the delegable.[16]

Probably one of the best arguments of Messrs. Hector and Minow is the concern that the persons who are engaged in rule making should properly keep themselves open to pressure, and yet at the same time must be kept insulated in matters of adjudication. Placing agency members in these incompatible positions tends to blur the rules of conduct for those who must deal with them and has created in some agencies a serious problem of *ex parte* communications. Of course, it is vitally important to the integrity of the process that the formal fact finding be kept free of *ex parte* communications by parties, but it should be noted that the primary fact-finding rests with the hearing examiners.

To meet the *ex parte* problem, some of the agencies [17] have recently adopted a formal code governing such conduct, which defines the persons who are engaged in the decision making process, draws the line between improper and proper communications with those persons at the commencement of a formal proceeding, and establishes a procedure for disclosing on the record any improper communications.*

* * *

Let me repeat my initial thesis: administrative agencies were designed to formulate and carry out comprehensive regulatory programs for particular industries or segments of the economy. At least in the case of the SEC and agencies having like problems, both rule making and adjudication are necessary tools for effective regulation. To divorce the adjudicatory from the rule making

---

* The *ex parte* communications problem is not, I confess, a matter of consequence to the SEC. Unlike some of the other regulatory agencies, it is not dealing with an industry consisting of a small number of large units. As it does not award valuable monopoly rights to particular business entities, the pressures on the members may be somewhat lessened.

[16] See Nathanson, *Looking Backward: 2000–1963: A Personal View of the Administrative Conference*, 1961–62, 16 ADM. L. REV. 33, 37–38 (1963).
[17] See SEC *Code of Behavior Governing Ex Parte Communications Between Persons Outside the Commission and Decisional Employees*, 17 C.F.R. § 200.111–114.

and administrative functions would fragment the regulatory responsibility and deprive both the adjudicators and the rule makers of the valuable feedback between the two regulatory processes.

In my view, the goals sought by Mr. Hector and Mr. Minow—effective policy making and improvement of standards of quality and fairness in administrative adjudication—can best be achieved through existing agency structures. Good management, not radical transformation, is the avenue to improvement of the administrative process.

### Alternatives

If we accept the position that the judicial function should not be divorced from regulatory agencies, then what alternative steps should be taken to improve them? First of all, I have already emphasized the Landis suggestion that there should be more delegation—better management—so that the commission is in a better posture to focus its attention on policy.

In addition, in order to get anything done I believe a commission should be smaller, having a maximum of five (perhaps three) commissioners, and further that there must be a chairman designated by the President. I deplore a recommendation made by President Kennedy that the Federal Power Commission should be enlarged so that it could meet in panels to clear up its backlog of work.[18] Indeed, this would have had exactly the opposite effect, and would have moved in the direction of the ICC. Happily, this suggestion was not adopted. With better management under the direction of Chairman Swidler, the underlying problems of the FPC were faced and resolved. Further in this connection I believe that the panel system in the ICC should be abandoned. The question may be raised how that Commission could perform all of its assigned work; the present case load of the ICC is enormous. The answer is twofold: (1) some of its work might and should be eliminated and this subject should have priority on the Commission agenda; and (2) responsibility for both initial decision and review can be even further vested in

---

[18] President Kennedy, Special Message on Regulatory Agencies to the 87th Cong., 1st Sess. (April 13, 1961), p. III B(2).

panels of career civil servants, with a form of certiorari left in the Commission itself. The FCC Review Board, mentioned in Chapter 3, is said to have proven successful. A system must be developed by which a smaller commission may focus upon the major policy issues before it.

As to limiting the membership of commissions, an argument can be made in some cases for a single head of a regulatory commission. Probably the best vehicle for such a proposal is the Atomic Energy Commission, which is essentially an operating agency differing more from the six commissions here discussed than from some government bureaus or departments.[19] The idea has been suggested by President Johnson, but never formally proposed.

Finally, as already indicated in Chapter 3, I believe a perfectly balanced Commission or an overjudicialized one is unlikely to provide a vigorous administration.

The reference to the work of the ICC in the preceding paragraph raises the question of coordination among agencies. Obviously this whole problem is beyond the scope of this book. It is clear, however, that there is a desperate need for both initiative and coordination in the field of transportation. It may now, properly, become a public issue through the President's 1966 recommendation of a new Department of Transportation.[20] Any movement in this direction will, of course, inevitably have some effect upon the role of the ICC, the CAB, and the Federal Maritime Administration, and may indeed portend the ultimate curtailment of their functions. In view of the jealous attitude of Congress toward these agencies, the proposal of a department at Cabinet level seems much wiser than the suggestion of a czar within the White House. Chapter 1 has demonstrated that these bodies are regarded as "arms of Congress" and the czar approach would be politically fatal.

We then come to the question of independence of an agency. In view of the attitude of Congress and of some commissions and commission chairmen, it seems clear that some "independence"

---

[19] See BERMAN & HYDEMAN, THE ATOMIC ENERGY COMMISSION AND REGULATING NUCLEAR FACILITIES (Univ. of Mich. 1961), p. 239ff.

[20] See Chap. 2, p. 34.

from the White House actually exists. It is a relative term, but is not entirely myth. Of course, there may be comparable freedom in some executive bureaus and departments. As Professor Bernstein has pointed out,[21] "Single-headed departments and agencies or their subdivisions may in fact be substantially independent of presidential direction when a highly organized interest group exercises strong clientele influence over the agency or bureau." A case in point is the Corps of Engineers of the Army in handling river and harbor projects dear to Congress. Furthermore, independence within an executive department varies widely in accordance with the person holding office. As with commissioners, discussed in Chapter 1, much depends upon his own ambition, philosophy, status, reputation, and personal standards. If the official is *persona grata* to the interests with which he deals on the one hand, or has demonstrated capacity and courage on the other, the prospect of removing him can be quite embarrassing even though presidential power clearly exists.

The relationship with the White House and Congress represents a tension among forces in the regulation of business. It has its counterpart in the securities industry: self-regulation is an attempt to strike a balance between regulatory power vested in the exchanges and the NASD, and control in turn by the SEC and ultimately by Congress. Indeed, both examples illustrate the dilemma of maintaining social control despite decentralization in a pluralistic, democratic, society.

The justifications for and the weaknesses of "independence" in the regulatory agencies were brilliantly analyzed in Professor Bernstein's book some ten years ago. In his opinion the case for independence logically seems to rest on unsound ground. And yet he concluded that the real difficulty lies not in fitting the programs of independent commissions into national economic policy but rather in developing national policy itself.

Recognizing all the imperfections in the theory of independence, I am content to see the "myth" preserved. I have attempted to describe its metes and bounds by specific example rather than broad principle. Whether or not the principle of autonomy is questionable, the political justification remains strong.

[21] BERNSTEIN, *op. cit.*, p. 146.

In fact, Bernstein says [22] some regulatory agencies would probably not exist at all if they were not independent. Furthermore, the practical alternatives are not entirely palatable. On the one hand, these agencies might be poured into the Department of Commerce, already a brew—indeed a bouillabaisse—of unrelated activities. On the other hand, they might be made directly subordinate to the White House—in actual fact, to the presidential assistants of the second tier.

It is true, as already noted, that there may be more agencies doing regulatory work under executive departments which are not independent. Yet it does not follow that the commissions involved in regulation of business should not be "independent." So long as they are large and important enough to warrant actual oversight by Congress and the White House I believe there is some basis for their remaining autonomous. At the same time, I do not feel that freedom need be total. The White House should assert itself to ensure that the agencies are functioning effectively and set the course on which they are to proceed.

The power of Congress has already been demonstrated in Chapter 2. We have seen, by example, evidence that it may prevent a commission from taking action and indeed may paralyze it through extended congressional investigation or hearing. It may subconsciously or unconsciously frustrate any possibility of vigorous administration by insisting upon a large commission and a rotating chairman, as in the case of the ICC. It may thwart commission proposals, as in the case of the FCC. Where legislation is proposed or enacted, obviously Congress is omnipotent and autocratic. Despite the criticism frequently leveled at Congress, we must not forget that it is performing an essential role vis-a-vis the regulatory agency. It may be the principal factor in keeping the commission from dying of inertia. Oversight by Congress is sometimes wearing, almost unendurable, but it is an integral part of the system.

I do not believe it is fair to conclude that agencies are not responsive to the public, or as some may say, "responsible to no one." As already indicated, there are many forces at work on them, notably Congress and the White House, and the industries

[22] *Ibid.*, p. 148.

under their jurisdiction. Whenever there is an outcry by companies that are regulated, congressional committees and their staffs are ready to look into the situation. Generally, I believe as many different pressures should be at work upon a commission as possible. For that reason, I never objected to the intrusion of the Anti-Trust Division of the Department of Justice into the jurisdiction of the SEC and would welcome in principle the roving investigator for government agencies such as the ombudsman, which has been proposed in a House bill and has been widely discussed by Professor Walter Gellhorn.[23] The only trouble is that since people are apt to complain more vigorously when an agency does something than when it merely stands still, an ombudsman might increase the already excessive pressures toward inertia.

As to further remedies to meet the problems of the agencies, I would return to the wisdom of Judge Friendly. He has found a deep-seated need for more planning and policy making on the part of agencies. To achieve this he offers several suggestions. He says the best agency to improve performance is the agency itself; and accepts the view that the President should ensure that the commissions function but not undertake to tell them how. With this general thesis I generally concur, and have tried to pursue it throughout these chapters. He also believes we need better people in the agencies. With this, of course, no one can disagree, but it bears repetition.[24]

Further, he suggests that responsibility for regulatory agencies lies with Congress, recommending that each committee should be under the obligation each ten or fifteen years to render a comprehensive report, with specific proposals for amendment or with a considered statement that none is required.[25] Though sympathetic, I have great reservations in practice though not in theory. I do not believe that Congress is capable of serving as the energizing force with respect to the agencies. The responsibility

---

[23] Full discussion is available in Professor Gellhorn's Holmes Lectures, delivered at Harvard University in 1966 and published by the Harvard University Press under the title "When Americans Complain." See "Ombudsman and All That," 68 HARV. ALUMNI BULL. 584 (May 7, 1966).

[24] See Smith, *Recent Trends in the Appointment of Commissioners,* 13 OHIO ST. L.J. 479 (1952).

[25] FRIENDLY, *op. cit.,* at 172.

should rest upon the chairman and commissioners, who should be charged by statute with making a detailed periodic report to Congress on industry developments and their effect upon future regulation, and with setting forth any legislative proposals that are called for. The commission may have to go to Congress to obtain an appropriation for such studies to be made, although I believe both the funds and the authorization should be automatic. But if it does not take such action, and does not take the further responsibility for delegating subsidiary questions so that the agency itself may concentrate upon policy, nothing will happen. I accept Mr. Landis' view [26] that the chairman is the focal point, though I recognize that he can be helped immeasurably, and in turn be prodded if he has such able colleagues as I was fortunate to have.

Finally, Judge Friendly suggests that law teachers and reviews may perform a useful role. He says they have not yet begun to do for administrative agencies what they have been doing for the courts.[27] As a member of the guild, I cannot approach his suggestion with complete objectivity. Suffice it to say, the material in this book does not purport to be the work of a teacher-scholar objectively surveying the battle from a tower, but impressions of one who has been in the trenches, or more precisely in one of them.

I come back to the ambivalent conclusion that "independent" agencies are not truly independent and yet there is substance in the myth. They are part of government and, indeed, small governments within themselves.[28] I recall the question that was asked me after I had been in the SEC a month: Who is going to act as your liaison with Congress? The answer should be and was that the chairman is his own liaison. Whether he likes it or not, as the head of an agency he is in politics.[29]

---

[26] *Landis Report*, pp. 12, 37.

[27] FRIENDLY, *op. cit.*, at 174.

[28] See Loevinger, *The Administrative Agency as a Paradigm of Government: A Survey of the Administrative Process*, 40 IND. L.J. 287 (1965).

[29] See Jaffe, *The Effective Limits of the Administrative Process: A Reevaluation*, 67 HARV. L. REV. 1105 (1954).

# Index

141

142

143

145

146

147

148

Securities markets, market makers, 96, 111
   prior to 1934, 6
   self-regulation, 71, 76, 108, 136
   situation leading toward "Special Study", 71
Self-regulation, Department of Justice attitude, 99
   failure and reform, 72–73
   limitations, 43–45
   in mutual fund companies, 81
   within regulatory agencies, 139
   in securities industry, 71, 76, 108, 136
Senate Appropriations Committee, 36
Senate Banking Committee, 35–36
Senate Committee on Government Operations, 29–30
Smith, H. W., 119
Smoking (see Cigarette smoking)
Special Study of the Securities Markets, 16, 18
   appropriations, problems of, 92
   controversy in Congress, 93
   coverage, 75
   differences of opinion within SEC, 66
   House hearings on Report, 107
   inception, 71
   insurance companies, 113
   legislative history, 92
   results, 75–78
   techniques employed, 130
States' rights, in insurance industry, 113–114
   problems of SEC bill, 107–108

Stock exchange (see New York Stock Exchange; Securities markets)
Surveys, 78–79
Swidler, J. C., 9, 62–63, 65

Television, all channel receiver, 49–50
   subscription television, controversy, 47–49
   UHF (ultra high frequency) controversy, 49
   (See also Broadcasting industry)
Texas Gulf Sulphur Co., 18
Thomas, Albert, 36, 92
"To prosecute or not to prosecute," 18
Tobacco industry, 53–55
Transportation, ICC conflicts, 34
   proposed Department of Federal government, 34–35, 135
Truman, Harry S.,
   attitude toward ICC, 32
   relation to regulatory agencies, 6

United States Chamber of Commerce, 95

Weiner, J. L., 70
Wenzell, Adolphe, 13–14
White, L. C., 63
White House (see President, The)
Williams, H. A., 30

149